MRS LUTHER AND HER SISTERS

"This is an original and captivating work, with all the hallmarks of excellence we have come to expect of Derek Wilson, who is one of the finest historians of our times. This is an area few have explored, so this book is a valuable addition to sixteenth-century scholarship."

ALISON WEIR, author and historian

"The Reformation (and Counter-Reformation) opened up new pathways, not only to heaven, but also for women in society. Mrs Luther and Her Sisters is a timely and absorbing study of the sometimes mutually beneficial relationship between women and the Reformation in early modern Europe – a fascinating parade of fierce and faithful ladies."

JESSIE CHILDS, author and historian

"When we think of the Reformation the names that spring to mind are Martin Luther, John Calvin, and Huldrych Zwingli – all men. We think of the women of the time as simply homemakers submitting to their husbands and not having any real role in the religious changes sweeping Europe in the sixteenth century, but renowned historian Derek Wilson corrects this view. Mrs Luther and Her Sisters combines Wilson's meticulous research with his gift for storytelling to bring the women of the Reformation out of the shadows and into the limelight. Women played crucial roles in the Reformation, as disseminators of new religious ideas, as prophets, as patrons, as educators, as founders of religious establishments, and also, unfortunately, as victims of religious persecution and as persecutors. The women of the Reformation had a huge impact on their society yet this has been overlooked until now. Bravo Derek Wilson!"

CLAIRE REYNOLDS, Founder of the Tudor Society and The Anne Boleyn Files, and Tudor history author

Also by Derek Wilson

The People's Bible

The English Reformation

Reformation (with Felipe Fernandez Armesto)

A Tudor Tapestry

Charlemagne

Out of the Storm – The Life and Legacy of Martin Luther

Hans Holbein – Portrait of an Unknown Man

The King and the Gentleman – Charles Stuart and Oliver Cromwell

Magnificent Malevolence

MRS LUTHER AND HER SISTERS

WOMEN IN THE REFORMATION

Derek Wilson

LION

Published by Lion Books
an imprint of
Lion Hudson plc
Wilkinson House, Jordan Hill Road,
Oxford OX2 8DR, England
www.lionhudson.com/lion

Paperback ISBN 978 0 7459 5640 4
Hardback ISBN 978 0 7459 5635 0
e-ISBN 978 0 7459 5793 7

First edition 2016

Acknowledgments

pp. 16, 26, 36, 37, 153: *Here I Stand : A Life of Martin Luther* © R. Bainton, 1987.
Copyright ©1991 by Abingdon Press. Used by permission. All rights reserved.

pp. 23, 24, 25, 28, 208: *Luther on Women: A Sourcebook* © S. C. Karant-Nunn and
M. E. Wiesner-Hanks, 2003. Used by permission of Cambridge University Press.

pp. 34, 35, 68, 71, 87, 93, 94, 95, 96, 97, 101, 112, 114, 130, 132, 133, 138, 143: *Women
of the Reformation: In Germany and Italy* © R. Bainton, 1971, 2007. Used by permission of
Augsburg Fortress Publishers.

pp. 34, 54, 139: *Reformation: Europe's House Divided* 1490–1700 by Diarmaid MacCulloch
(Penguin Books, 2004) Copyright © Diarmaid MacCulloch, 2003.

pp. 37, 122, 123: *Women Writers of the Renaissance and Reformation* © K. M. Wilson, 1987.
Used by permission of University of Georgia Press.

pp. 49, 61–62: *Caritas Pirckheimer: A Journal of the Reformation Years 1524–1528* © P. A.
MacKenzie (trans.), 2006. Used by permission of Boydell and Brewer.

pp. 60, 118, 119, 155, 156, 203: *Profiles of Anabaptist Women: Sixteenth-Century
Reforming Pioneers*, A. C. Snyder and L. A. H. Hecht, 1996. Used with kind permission
of Wilfrid Laurier University Press.

p. 63: *Converts Confront the Reformation: Catholic and Protestant Nuns in Germany* © Merry
Wiesner-Hanks (ed.), Joan Skocir (trans.), 1996. Used by permission of Marquette
University Press.

pp. 76, 77, 82, 86: *Women of the Reformation: In France and England* © R. Bainton, 2007.
Used by permission of Augsburg Fortress Publishers.

pp. 88, 131, 109, 132, 143: *Women and the Reformation* © K. Stjerna, 2009. Used by
permission of John Wiley and Sons.

A catalogue record for this book is available from the British Library

Printed and bound in Poland, February 2016, LH44

CONTENTS

Introduction

It is usual in a work of historical critique for the writer to set out his/her evidence, to interpret that evidence and, finally, to draw all the threads together tidily in a chapter of "conclusions". The problem with the present subject is that it is made up of a large number of interlinked strands. To change the metaphor, the journey on which we are about to embark is not one which starts at A and passes through B, C, D, etc. on its way to Z. It has more of the nature of a ramble. We shall set off down winding lanes, encounter several crossroads, and sometimes find ourselves revisiting familiar landmarks but approaching from a different direction. Occasionally, we shall come to a dead end and be obliged to retrace our steps. As if that were not complicated enough, the landscape we journey through is war-torn – disfigured with shattered villages and ravaged farms. So, because we are dealing with conflicting ideologies in an age of social dislocation, I believe it will be helpful to set out my conclusions in advance – a guidebook, if you will, to the chapters which follow.

Our subject is Reformation women. It immediately breaks down into two subordinate questions: what contributions did women make to the Reformation? And how did the Reformation affect the position of women in society?

The contributions of women to the Reformation

In late medieval Europe, the vast majority of women were either homemakers or nuns. No one doubted that, in the divine ordering of society, women were subservient to men. They were under the governance of their fathers until such time as they were married (which might occur at any time after the onset of puberty). Thereafter, they were at the beck and call of their husbands and were expected to care for them, and to bear and nurture their children. Unmarried women were a burden on their families and communities and, for this reason, many widows and virgins were placed in the cloister. That is not to say that none experienced a genuine call to the life of prayer. Society had always had a special regard for female visionaries, ecstatics, and prophets, but such holy women were rare. The sisters tended to come from families who paid the convents to "take them off their hands" and provide them with an honourable, safe, and meaningful environment. It was in the nunneries that the majority of literate and semi-literate women were to be found. Their knowledge of Latin and written vernaculars exposed them to the new ideas of the reformers. Senior members of convents also acquired administrative skills, responsible, as they were, for dealing with tradesmen, overseeing labourers, and running landed estates. It is no surprise to find that, once freed from convent life, many of these ex-nuns played a prominent part in the early Reformation.

Another smaller, though very significant, group of women were the intellectuals. Renaissance humanism, with its emphasis on education as a vital part of the virtuous life, re-evaluated the social position of women. Juan Luis Vives, Erasmus, Thomas More, and other advanced thinkers advocated study, particularly for the female members of aristocratic and royal households, asserting that girls were just as capable as their brothers of improving their minds. The early sixteenth century produced a number of female celebrities who were hailed as remarkable because of their grasp of scholarly principles. Some corresponded on equal terms with the leading intellectuals of the age. It was inevitable that such bold spirits would engage in the Reformation debate.

The advent of vernacular Scriptures accelerated this phenomenon and spread it down the social scale. When women, as well as men, learned to read, they shared their insights with one another, through letters, pamphlets, and hymns. Their contributions to the life of local churches and the Reformation movement as a whole were, in the early years, welcomed. The participation of women tended to be more pronounced among the new radical groups (usually bracketed together as "Anabaptists"), which laid emphasis on the work of the Holy Spirit, who, they believed, did not restrict his revelations to men.

A third group of women who were important (in some instances, crucially important) to the spread of the Reformation were those who exercised political power or influence. In an age when state religions were established by government decree, to achieve the conversion of a ruling queen or duchess or even a royal consort was a considerable coup. The conduct of heresy trials was the business of the church but those found guilty were handed over to the secular arm for punishment. It was, therefore, territorial rulers who decided how far persecution would be allowed to go. Reformers were diligent in canvassing the support of royal and ducal wives and mothers – and, indeed, of any female courtiers who were perceived to wield influence.

There remains one more female category to be considered. Few of its members became famous. In fact, most of their names are unknown. But their importance would be impossible to exaggerate. They were clergy wives. No such creatures had existed in Europe before. Priests were celibate. When nunneries closed, the marriage market was flooded with eligible ladies (and ladies who needed support). At the same time, Protestant theology rejected the Catholic concept of celibate priesthood. All the Reformation leaders were united in encouraging Christian ministers to take wives. There thus came into being a whole new social category – the clergy helpmeet. Because this phenomenon was new, there were no conventions governing the behaviour of the parson's wife. Some regarded themselves as joint pastors with their husband. Those who remained in the background exercised a considerable influence as educators of their own and their neighbours' children.

If women now had more opportunities to contribute to the life of their churches and to live out their faith, they were also able to die for their faith. Many did so, in increasing numbers. Some perished alongside their Christian brethren in mob massacres or in purges instigated by the Inquisition. Others were singled out for special attention by outraged ecclesiastical authorities, not only for the beliefs they expressed but also because, as mere women, they had the temerity to express any beliefs at all. Nor was it only the representatives of the "old religion" who persecuted those committed to unorthodox doctrines. Though the vast majority of heretics consigned to the flames were murdered at the instigation of Catholic tribunals, some were hounded by mainstream Protestants. The founders of Lutheran, Calvinist, and Anglican separatist movements were anxious to dissociate themselves from the more radical elements of the Reformation movement. The new freedom of religious thought and expression was not limitless, and "respectable" Protestant regimes did not shrink from imposing the death penalty on those who, for example, rejected the divinity of Christ. The "Anabaptist" communities could boast a comparatively high percentage of female martyrs and that was because, in these less-inhibited extremist communities, women played a more prominent role. Some of the more harrowing accounts of public burnings are those which feature the sufferings of women (sometimes pregnant women) martyrs.

Women thus fulfilled a variety of novel functions in the first decades of the Reformation. As the old shackles of Catholic dogma were struck off, it seemed that women would also be set free from the social restrictions that had bound their foremothers. They taught, they preached, they conducted public worship, they debated Christian truth with the leading scholars of the age, they wrote books, they took part in missionary endeavour. In short, they were among the celebrities of the sixteenth century. They were feminists *avant la lettre*.

The position of women in society

For twenty or, perhaps, thirty years, European womankind benefited from the shake-up of society of which the Reformation was both a cause and a symptom. The new churches needed inspiring and inspired contributions from all those who had the courage and conviction to stand up and be counted, casting convention aside. In this "brave new world", many gained recognition for their spiritual and intellectual qualities. Gender issues took a back seat. Did the surge of proto-feminism lead to permanent social change? No. As the century passed its halfway point, age-old norms reasserted themselves. Tentative steps in the direction of sexual equality faltered. Male domination staked its claim once more.

As far as religious life is concerned, there were two reasons for this. National Protestant churches established themselves only with the support of secular powers. Secular powers cherished stability above all things. They were not going to see that threatened by emancipated women standing shoulder to shoulder with men in the councils of the church. The other reason was the testimony of

Scripture. The open Bible had powered the Reformation. From its pages female activists – with the support of some theologians – had drawn the principle that men and women are equal in the sight of God. But, in the changed circumstances of the 1540s and 1550s, this truth was brought under closer scrutiny. Men and women might be – certainly were – equal heirs of salvation but that did not mean that they were designed to perform the same functions in the household of God. In the very beginning women had been designated as playing a supporting role to men, and the apostle Paul had made it clear that women should be silent in church and submit to their husbands in matters of doctrine. The word of God, therefore, provided justification for the male domination of society.

But the past always plants its footprints on the present. It was impossible for the realignment of gender roles during the first phase of the Reformation not to have an ongoing influence. During the years and decades that followed, women retreated into the background – or so the records suggest. With very few exceptions, they did not write or preach or campaign or lead congregations. But their influence becomes clear once we look beneath the surface. More and more of them acquired education. In particular, they studied the Bible. A seventeenth-century visitor to England noted that some women took notes during sermons and, later, discussed them with their domestics. The fundamental building block of society was the home and this was the domain of wives and mothers. The influence of devout women on their children and servants – and, therefore, on the wider society – cannot be overestimated. And, naturally, the "goodwives" of a neighbourhood met together – not merely to gossip, but to discuss ideas and read the Bible. Such groups (in Germany known as *Frauenzimmer*) were common.

But the most long-lasting change was the one instituted by Martin Luther and Catherine von Bora in 1524. From that time a fixed feature of all Protestant churches was the married clergyman. Right across northern Europe and, from there, in all lands where non-Catholic Christianity put down roots, women would be found alongside their husbands, often involved in teaching and pastoral activity, but always patterning the Christian home.

CHAPTER 1

DR AND MRS LUTHER

Philip Melanchthon was stunned. His old friend, associate, and idol, Martin Luther, had done something incredibly stupid. Writing to a friend in the summer of 1525, he reported that he was completely at a loss to explain the pioneer reformer's action: "In these unhappy times, in which good people are suffering so much, this man lacks compassion and rather, as it seems, revels and compromises his good reputation, precisely at a time when Germany stands in particular need of his spirit and authority."[1] What grievous error had Luther fallen into? He had got married. Melanchthon was affronted, not because he disapproved of the institution of wedlock, nor because he was surprised that Luther was in favour of it. Both men had virulently opposed clerical celibacy. There was no *theological* reason why Luther should not take a wife. What annoyed Melanchthon was the timing of this event.

Germany was in chaos. A widespread revolt by the lower orders had mushroomed into what history knows as the Peasants' War, and the evangelical movement was unavoidably caught up in it. Insurrectionist preachers took the liberty of the gospel and turned it into a manifesto for bloody social change. As villages burned, houses were looted and landowners exacted hideous revenge on the rebels, leaders on both sides looked to Luther for support. Melanchthon was not alone among reforming pastors and preachers in believing that their prime responsibility was to pour oil on the raging waters of civil unrest. A long-standing supporter expressed the opinion of many when he heard rumours of their wedding: "If this monk takes a wife, the whole world and the Devil himself will laugh and all the work he has done for now will have been for nought."[2] Even committed reformers found it difficult to disentangle themselves from ancient orthodoxies concerning sexual relations.

For more than a thousand years, neoplatonic asceticism had provided the philosophical ground rules for the Christian understanding of human nature. Man was made up of *sarx* and *pneuma*, flesh and spirit. Anyone who sought holiness would strive to free him-/herself from "bondage" to the flesh. Monks, nuns, and priests were (theoretically) those who had chosen the path of abstinence in order to escape from worldly taint. Carnal desire was a satanic temptation. God permitted it for lay people within marriage, but strictly for the procreation of children. Thomas Aquinas had insisted that indulging in the sex act for the giving or receiving of pleasure, even within marriage, was fornication. A chaste life was something that set the priest apart from ordinary mortals and enabled him to be a means of mediation between God and man. In theory. Notoriously, abstention was practised more in the breach than the observance. Everyone knew this, but reality was not allowed to get in the way of theory. If the "otherness" of priests was ever to be called in doubt, then men might go on to question their sacerdotal function. The entire Catholic system of confession, absolution, and performance of the priestly miracle might be shaken.

In this Luther took his stand, as in all other issues, on the rock of Holy Scripture. As early as 1520, when he dramatically defied papal authority by making a bonfire of many Catholic books, he explained his action in a treatise pointing out the errors emanating from Rome. One such error was: "No-one who is married is able to serve God, even though Abraham and many saints have been married and God himself established marriage."[3] He consistently took his stand on Genesis 2:18: "It is not good that man should be alone. I will make him a helper." What God had arranged as a fundamental component of human society, no pope had the authority to unarrange.

For Luther, experience as well as Scripture proved that, for those seeking holiness, pursuing the monastic path was a cul-de-sac. His revolt against traditional teaching began with his bitter frustration at not being able to achieve righteousness by his own efforts. It followed that the celibate life, far from being the highest vocation for a Christian man or woman, was no vocation at all. God called each and every one of them to a specific role, so that the tailor or the milkmaid, faithfully carrying out their allotted tasks, were being as true to their vocation as the diligent priest. Moreover, God had created male and female with inbuilt desires, and the suppression of those desires could have only unfortunate consequences. Nevertheless, Luther remained single. He did not even abandon his monastic vows until 1524. The fact that God had ordained marriage did not mean that every Christian had to be married, and he felt no pull in that direction himself. When he was asked why he did not practise what he preached, Luther replied that it would not be fair to involve a woman in his dangerous and highly stressful life. Hence the shock that went through the evangelical churches when, only a year later, he took to wife Catherine von Bora.

The series of events that culminated in this volte-face were little short of sensational. The members of several male and female orders who had been won over to reformed religion had left their convents and become members of lay society. For most men this change of lifestyle was not too much of a problem;

they had families or local communities who could help them find employment. Women – and particularly women of some social standing – were not as fortunate. Most of them had a stark choice: marriage or the nunnery. And their decisions were dictated by economic rather than religious considerations. Daughters of landed families existed for the purpose of making advantageous alliances. A father wishing to see his girls married to "suitable" spouses had to provide them with tempting dowries. If he could not afford to do so and if he did not want to feed and clothe them in perpetuity, he would place them in a convent. For a modest down payment, the holy sisters would take a girl off her family's hands at an early age and attend to her material and spiritual needs. In this way, religious houses were provided with financial support and also a pool of potential novices. Not all girls in nunneries espoused the religious life. For some the convent was merely a single-sex hostel where they could live chastely and in reasonable comfort. This, of course, did not banish their natural desires, a fact which gave rise to numerous scurrilous tales (some undoubtedly true) of "goings-on" within the cloistered precincts. Most young women doubtless preserved their virtue, but with varying degrees of reluctance. So, when Luther and his friends, in their books and sermons, condemned monastic life, some nuns as well as monks espied a welcome escape route.

One night in April 1523, twelve nuns of the Cistercian convent at Nimbschen in Saxony literally "escaped". A local merchant who provided the sisters with herrings and who was, therefore, allowed in, smuggled the women out in his cart. The escapade was masterminded by Luther. It was risky because the abduction of nuns was a capital offence, but the cargo was safely delivered to Wittenberg and lodged in the Augustinian priory where Luther continued to live. One of those nuns was the twenty-four-year-old Catherine von Bora.

Catherine's father was of the minor nobility, with estates near Leipzig. She had received a good basic education in a Benedictine cloister before being sent to Nimbschen at the age of nine or ten. Her family had close connections with the house and two of her aunts were of the sisterhood. We can imagine her leading a genteel life with forty or so other women and girls of noble breeding throughout her teenage years when she was not expected to submit to the full rigours of a contemplative life. However, the time came when she would have either to leave or to take religious vows. In all probability, the decision was made for her by her father and stepmother. She took the veil at the age of sixteen. Thus, from her birth to her mid-twenties, Catherine had no real experience of the outside world. But she could read and she could discuss what she read with her colleagues. They were a coterie of cultured, aristocratic ladies who took an interest in the theological debates which, from about 1520, were raging with increasing ferocity. Presumably, they were not supposed to be allowed access to the works of radicals and heretics, such as Martin Luther, but such dangerous material did come into their hands. Catherine was among the rebels who sent messages to Wittenberg begging for their release.

Once he had accepted responsibility for the Nimbschen ladies, what was Luther to do with them? The answer was to marry them off to his respectable friends and co-religionists. This he was able to do with no apparent difficulty. Except for Catherine von Bora. A year later she was still on his hands. The basic reason seems to have lain in Catherine's character. She was a strong-willed woman who was determined to marry a man of *her* choice. Up to now, her way of life had been decided for her by her father. She was not about to leap from the frying pan into the fire. She was very conscious of her own aristocratic status and would only contemplate marriage with a man she considered worthy of her. Soon after her arrival in Wittenberg she fell in love with someone who came up to her expectations. Hieronymus Baumgartner was about the same age as her, was one of Luther's students, and came from a good family. He returned her affection and they discussed marriage. But when Hieronymus reported to his family, they quickly scotched the romance and found him a younger – and wealthier – bride. Catherine watched all her erstwhile sisters settle into comfortable domesticity. This must have had some influence on her. She was currently in limbo. She could not continue to live in the Wittenberg cloister as a single woman but she was too proud to have any man foisted on her as a husband. Melanchthon believed – and it has been accepted as part of the story ever since – that Catherine set her cap at Luther and made all the running in their "courtship". If she did take the initiative it was probably with the understandable conviction that the man who was determining her destiny should be prepared to become personally involved in it.

On Luther's part, his affections were engaged by another of the Nimbschen maidens. But he, too, was destined to be disappointed when the lady in question married a local apothecary. Evidently his reluctance to espouse the married state was wearing thin. One reason was pressure from home. His father had always opposed Martin's monastic vocation. He wanted his son to marry and provide him with grandchildren. Now that Martin was free (and not getting any younger!), there was no reason why he should not do his filial duty. So the old man reasoned, and his continued pestering had its effect. Another argument also weighed with the reformer: how could he urge other ex-monks to marry as a gesture of defiance to Rome if he was not prepared to set an example? He decided – as a matter of duty – that he would marry Catherine. When writing to a friend he was anxious to point out (in words which may seem to us ungallant) that this was God's doing, "for I feel neither passionate love nor burning desire for my spouse".[4]

It may be that we should take with a slight pinch of salt Luther's claim to immunity from sexual desire. Not only did he reject the Catholic theologians' neoplatonic spirituality, which asserted perpetual warfare between "flesh" and "spirit", he actually revelled in his God-given human nature. Hearing him talk quite openly later about his intimate relations with Katie must have made some of his friends wince. Writing to his friend Georg Spalatin to congratulate him on his wedding, he urged him to embrace his bride eagerly, thanking God that this wonderful creature had been given to him by Christ, and he made a personal promise: "On the evening of the day on which … you will receive this, I shall make love to my Catherine while you make love to yours, and thus we will be united in love."[5] Many of the reformer's friends and colleagues were never able to shake off their unease about this seemingly bizarre attitude. Whatever the reasons behind the union of Martin and Catherine, they plighted their troth to each other in a low-key ceremony on 13 June 1525. It was to prove one of the most significant marriages in European history.

What Catherine found in the old Augustinian cloister at Wittenberg was Luther, one other ex-monk, and a bevy of servants rattling around in the extensive monastic buildings. Luther's old patron, Duke Frederick (who had recently died), had given permission for him to remain in the convent but he had no idea how to maintain the draughty old building, let alone how to find new uses for the accommodation and the grounds. Catherine had her work cut out to establish a viable domestic economy, especially as her husband received only a very modest stipend as a lecturer at Wittenberg University. She responded to the challenge with a will. The conventual buildings had to be turned into a home. Catherine designed a new entrance. She had a well dug. The old monastic cells were turned into student digs. Catherine competed with other landladies by undercutting their board and lodging prices and cashing in on her husband's fame. Many undergraduates were attracted by the opportunity to sit at table with the great Dr Luther. Catherine made full use of the priory grounds. She cultivated vegetables and fruit and planted an orchard. She negotiated fishing rights in a local pond. She kept domestic animals on what amounted to a rapidly expanding smallholding. According to a tax return of 1542, she was rearing "five cows, nine calves, one goat with two kids, eight swine, two sows and three piglets".[6] Add to this the output of a well-regulated kitchen and it is clear that the household must have been virtually self-supporting. She had no hesitation about soliciting donations from wealthy friends or approaching landowners and businessmen who had embraced Lutheranism to finance the improvements. Within a few years the old, closed Augustinian house had become not just a home and a student hostel but also a meeting place for the local community, where parties and banquets were held – sometimes for as many as 130 guests.

Catherine was obviously an extremely able, practical woman. She lifted the domestic burden from Luther's shoulders and enabled him to concentrate on his teaching and writing. It took him little time to realize that he had been extremely fortunate in his choice of wife. And he was more than grateful. Whatever his feelings may have been before his marriage, there can be no doubt that they blossomed into a deep love. "My Katie is in all things so obliging and pleasing to me that I would not exchange my poverty for the riches of Croesus," Martin confided to a friend.[7] To another he affirmed, "I would not give my Katie for France and Venice together."[8] When Luther was away from home on family or pastoral business he never failed to write to his wife, and his letters, with their mix of cheerful banter, news, and practical concerns, give a vivid picture of a relationship which was a team affair:

God greet you in Christ, my Sweetheart Kate. I hope that if Doctor Buick gives me permission to leave … I will be able come with him tomorrow … Because Johannes [a servant] is moving away necessity and honour demands that I let him depart … in an honourable condition. For you know that he has served faithfully and diligently and humbly and truly kept to the gospel and done everything and suffered … So dip into your purse, and do not let such a pious fellow lack for anything … I am well aware that there is little there; but I would happily give him 10 gulden if I had it. But you should not give him less than 5 gulden … Whatever you are able to give him above that, I ask you do it … Think of where you get everything. God will provide you with more, that I know … I cannot find anything to buy for the children. If I do not bring anything special, have something on hand for me to give them … [9]

As this letter suggests, cash flow was often a problem. Catherine's task would have been easier (as she doubtless pointed out whenever the household budget struck rock bottom) had her husband been remotely interested in money and the management of money. The Luthers could have become extremely wealthy. Martin was by far the best-selling author in Europe. His numerous books and pamphlets were eagerly read throughout Germany and were translated into several languages. From all this success the author profited by not so much as one pfennig. When he had become a monk he had forsworn personal wealth, and he continued to believe that his God-given gifts should be used solely for the spread of the gospel and the edification of Christians, and not for his personal profit. Fortunately, Catherine was not so other-worldly. As well as soliciting gifts from wealthy friends and followers, she invested in property. After considerable argument with Martin, she bought from her brother a small estate at Zulsdorf and then went on to add to her portfolio a number of small parcels of land around Wittenberg.

It must sometimes have seemed to Catherine that her diligent husbandry amounted to little more than pouring money and effort into a sieve. Martin was generous to the point of profligacy. Generous and gullible. One day a certain "Rosina von Truchsess" appeared on the doorstep with a hard-luck story. She was, she said, a dispossessed nun with no means of livelihood. Against his wife's advice, Luther took her in and gave her a job in the household. His kindness was repaid with pilfering and covert prostitution and she was exposed only when she tried to obtain an abortion. The Luthers took no legal action against "Rosina" but, inevitably, after her dismissal, she revenged herself by spreading scurrilous rumours. As well as her husband's profligacy Catherine had to cope with the expenses of her large household and the maintenance of the conventual buildings, which must have soaked up funds like a sponge. However, she gradually won the battle of balancing income and expenditure.

Luther fully appreciated his wife's efficiency and allowed her considerable latitude in domestic matters, but his basic attitude towards her – and to all women – was completely in line with contemporary assumptions about the relative positions of the sexes. Several students who basked in the doctor's presence at the meal table made notes on his *obiter dicta*, which were later published in an anthology (*Luther's Table Talk*). Inevitably, these off-the-cuff remarks sometimes give an impression of inconsistency. Sometimes in his erudite conversation with students and colleagues in the theology faculty he made fun of his wife's lack of learning, calling her "Doctoress Catherine", but he was certainly not in favour of extending her theological education. He once amused his table companions with the aphorism "There is no dress that suits a woman ... so badly as wanting to be clever". On another occasion he expanded on this: while women's domestic expertise was beyond question, he asserted, "when they talk about matters other than those pertaining to the household, they are not competent ... For that reason they speak foolishly, without order, and wildly, mixing things together without moderation."[10] More tetchily, and speaking directly to his wife, he asserted, "The rule of women never accomplished anything good. God made Adam the lord of all creatures so that he might rule all living things. But when Eve persuaded him that he was lord above God, he thereby spoiled it all. We have that to thank you women for."[11] As in all things, it was to Scripture that Luther turned in support of his views on the subservience of women. But he also believed that physical distinctions implied the same. That seems to lie behind such laddish jokes as: "Men have broad chests and narrow hips, therefore they have wisdom ... Women ought to be domestic, the creation reveals it, for they have broad backsides and hips, so that they should sit still."[12]

In his teaching on the position of women we can discern the same tension that we see in other areas of Luther's theology. He was a revolutionary, trying to distance himself from social revolution. His marriage symbolized a fundamental change in the position of women in everyday life and it was an important step in the history of female emancipation, but he did not want to be seen to be dismantling the social fabric. He insisted that he was only restoring the biblical order of things. For all his theorizing, the reality of contented married life and his real admiration of Catherine's abilities constantly reminded him that his work for God would have been impossible without his wife's support. There is here a tension which he probably refused to admit to himself, but which we can glimpse in his letters to Catherine. For example, when he was asked to recommend a new pastor for the town of Greussen he involved her in the discussion during his absence: "As a clever lady and Mrs. Doctor you may help to advise Master George Maior and Master Ambrosio about which of the three whom I indicated ... may let himself be persuaded."[13]

Catherine was a mother as well as a wife and "domestic engineer". The Luthers' first child was born within a year of their marriage, to the delight of the father: "My dear Katie brought into the world yesterday by God's grace at two o'clock a little son," he wrote to a friend. "I must stop, sick Katie calls me."[14] Little Hans would be followed by five other siblings. Only one failed to survive infancy – something of a record for the mid-sixteenth century. This is a testimony to the loving care the children received from their parents. Again, it was Catherine who bore the main responsibility of bringing up the three boys and one girl who grew to full maturity (Magdalene died at the age of thirteen, to her parents' almost inconsolable grief). Martin was seldom out of the study or the lecture hall. When he was able to spend time with the children he tended to overcompensate and spoil them (and, of course, he was more of an age to be their grandfather than their father). However, there were holidays. These were not occasions when the family went away to visit relatives or see other places. They were literally "holy days", celebrations of major church feasts. As in everything else, Luther entered with gusto into such events. There were feasts, gift-giving, and games – and always there was music. Martin's love of singing and composing ensured that the whole household joined in the performance of sacred songs and hymns. One advantage the young Luthers had living in the student hostel was an abundant supply of "uncles", some of whom were employed to give the children their basic education. The fact that the siblings all went on to live successful – if undistinguished – lives suggests that their upbringing in the very unusual Wittenberg household served them well.

Katie had her hands full with Martin in more ways than one. Probably her greatest concern was for his health. He suffered, at various times, from several maladies – gout, insomnia, kidney stones, tinnitus, and constipation, to mention but a few. According to her son Paul, who qualified as a doctor, his mother was extremely well versed in herbal remedies and medical practices. She regulated her husband's diet, particularly restricting his consumption of wine. She regarded her own home-brewed beer as a more suitable beverage for someone with a weak stomach. But the greatest problem she had to cope with was one which no nostrums could assuage. Luther suffered from bouts of depression and these became worse with the passing of the years. It has often been remarked that the reformer's reputation would have fared better if he had died a few years earlier. The last decade of his life was marked by outbursts of anger and by works singularly lacking in charity (particularly, as has often been lamented, his condemnation of the Jews). He was disappointed that the church remained largely unreformed. Not only had the papacy shown its unwillingness to put its own house in order, but splits had appeared among reformed communities. He was overshadowed by a black cloud of personal failure. Even in Wittenberg Luther saw signs of apostasy. The townspeople, he grumbled on more than one occasion, "despise the Word of God, enter no church, hear no sermons, receive no sacrament. If they don't want to be Christians, let them be heathen, and for ever!"[15] The truth was that, while Luther's championing of Bible Christianity was still admired and applauded throughout much of Europe, in Germany his reputation had never recovered from the stance he had taken during the Peasants' War. The leaders had wanted to make him into a nationalist tub-thumper but he had sided with the landowners against anarchy. In parts of his homeland, Luther was yesterday's man. And in Wittenberg itself, as so often happens with local heroes, he had gone out of fashion. Citizens were now quite prepared to criticize the man they had once held in awe. Catherine had to bear her share of this disdain. Neighbours whispered behind her back about "those proud, hypocritical Luthers", who posed as champions of ordinary Christians against the might of the Roman church but who were merely using religion to enrich themselves.

Hard-headed business people are seldom popular. It was Catherine's lot to attract criticism and hostility. She gained a reputation for having ideas above her station. We cannot possibly assess how much truth there was in the complaints against her, but clearly she could not have achieved what she did without rubbing some people up the wrong way. As we have already seen, she was proud of her ancestry and she was certainly proud of her husband. Whether she liked it or not (and she probably did like it), she had celebrity status in and around Wittenberg. It would be understandable if, when she was in her element, dealing with servants and tradesmen, she asserted herself and, thus, appeared "pushy" and overbearing. As the economic anchor of the household she had to be a tough bargainer and forthright in negotiating with shopkeepers and market stallholders.

Luther was well aware of the hostility Catherine had to share. In his last years he became concerned about what would happen to her after his death. In one of his moments of depression he gave instruction for a move away from Wittenberg:

> *I wish that you would sell the garden and the field, house and yard. Then I would return the big house to my Most Gracious Lord [the Elector]. And it would be best for you if you moved to Zölsdorf while I am still living … Wittenburg will probably not tolerate you. For that reason it would be better to do what needs to be done while I am still alive …*[16]

In the winter of 1546, and the sixty-third year of his life, Luther set out for distant Eisleben to help settle a dispute in the family of a friend. He was accompanied by his three sons as well as his secretary. Catherine was left to look after the home in his absence. The weather was atrocious. The wagons made slow progress over the icy ruts and overflowing rivers. Although his health was deteriorating he refused to disappoint congregations along the way who wanted to hear him preach. Catherine knew the toll the journey would take and wrote to express her concerns. He replied on 7 February:

> *You seem determined to worry about me instead of letting God worry, as if he were not almighty and could not create ten Doctor Martins if the old one drowned in the Saale ... Free me from your worries. I have a caretaker who is better than you and all the angels: he lies in the cradle and rests on a virgin's bosom, and yet, nevertheless, he sits at the right hand of God, the Almighty father. Therefore be at peace, Amen ... Your little love, Martinus Luther.*[17]

He died two weeks later.

Catherine confided to a relative:

> *I am in truth so very saddened that I cannot express my great heartache to any person and do not know how I am and feel. I can neither eat nor drink. Nor again sleep. If I had owned a principality or empire I would not have felt as bad had I lost it, as I did when our dear Lord God took from me – and not only from me but from the whole world – this dear and worthy man.*[18]

As if her grief was not enough to bear, she had to fight the lawyers, who tried to change the terms of Luther's generous will. He had deliberately left her in charge of the Wittenberg ménage, with adequate funds to maintain the house and family. The law men did not share Luther's trust in Catherine and opposed this unconventional arrangement. But the redoubtable Catherine was more than a match for them. She outlived Martin by almost seven years and survived to see their sons established in their careers and her remaining daughter well married.

CHAPTER 2

WIVES AND MOTHERS

The relationship of Martin and Catherine Luther was, in its long-term impact, as revolutionary as the reformer's challenge to Rome and his Bible-based doctrine. Theirs was the prototype of the millions of clergy marriages which became the norm in Protestant lands. For the first time since the Fourth Lateran Council (1215) had reinforced clerical celibacy and erected a rigid barrier between laity and clergy, there were no longer three sexes in Europe – men, women, and priests. The family at the vicarage came to model Christian domestic life, based on love, mutual respect, and hospitality. Nothing underscored more clearly the change the Reformation introduced into daily life than the marriage of parish clergy. It altered the whole dynamic of relations between ordained and lay Christians. All Protestant churches abandoned the ancient teaching that sexual relations within marriage were, *ipso facto*, sinful, and that women were temptresses who would lure their husbands away from their duty to tend the flock of Christ.

The implications of this momentous shift in theological thinking did not win easy acceptance, however. Not until 1555 was the legal status of clergy wives and children recognized in the Holy Roman Empire. In England, Henry VIII and

Elizabeth I were both passionately opposed to clerical marriage. Thomas Cranmer, who as Archbishop of Canterbury helped Henry to disentangle himself from spiritual allegiance to the pope, found his susceptibility to female charms something of an embarrassment. During his Cambridge days he married a local girl. He married for love and was prepared to pay the price – the resignation of his fellowship. Had his young bride not died in childbirth, the course of the English Reformation (and, indeed, the whole of English history) would have been very different. Then, in 1532, while on a diplomatic mission in Germany, he married again, this time to a relative of the Nuremberg reformer Andreas Osiander. Theirs was not, and could not be, an open, pattern marriage, like the Luthers'. It was a clandestine affair, and remained so throughout most of Cranmer's life. Though he and Margaret had great affection for each other and produced children, Mrs Cranmer was kept hidden at one of the archbishop's houses far from the capital. It is inconceivable that Henry did not know of the relationship, but, since he had not embraced Lutheranism, he could not officially recognize it. It is ironical that, had Cranmer simply kept Margaret as his mistress, no one would have thought it worth mentioning, but the fact that he had a secret wife led to much sniggering among his enemies. The popular story went round that, when he moved from one residence to another, he transported Mrs Cranmer inside a coffer in which air holes had been drilled. Right down to the end of the century, bishops' wives were officially non-persons.

But the married pastor was not destined to be a transitory phenomenon, killed off by the disapproval of reactionaries. The wife/mother at the vicarage or manse became an accepted part of parish life, with a valued role. She partially filled the gap of "holy woman" left vacant by the disappearance of nuns and anchoresses. She supported her husband's ministry and frequently was an extension of it, providing a model of female virtue and offering advice and succour to the needy. The impact on society of this silent revolution was immense. Over time it created a whole new class. The family at the parsonage was poised between the people and the gentry. Like the gentry, the married clergy established influential dynasties, though few came close to the record established by William Barlow, Bishop of Chichester and companion in exile of Catherine and Richard Bertie (see below). His wife, Agatha, gave birth to five daughters. Each of them married a clergyman and each of those clergymen went on to become a bishop.

Most clergy wives were content with a domestic role but their "intermediate" position in the worlds of the ordained minister and the laity made it possible for educated women to extend their traditional roles and assert themselves in new ways if they were prepared to take the initiative. Nowhere was this more apparent than in Strasbourg. This, and not Wittenberg, was the location of the most vibrant and varied expressions of emergent Protestantism in the early years of the Reformation. Here audacious experiments in worship were carried out. Here men and women came seeking refuge from persecution in other towns, whether Catholic or Protestant. Strasbourg was a free imperial city. Because of its commercial importance, it enjoyed a measure of independence from both Vienna and Rome. The municipal council employed the leading clergy and increasingly selected them from the reformist camp. When it came to clergy marriages, Strasbourg was well in advance of Luther and his friends. All the leading clergy took wives. For this they were excommunicated, but, being supported by the municipal authorities, they were able to ignore all ecclesiastical sanctions. One of them was Matthew Zell, priest of the parish of St Lawrence, who, in December 1523, married Catherine Schütz (c.1497–1562), a local spinster.

From the beginning Catherine regarded herself as a partner in ministry, and her husband endorsed her commitment. Professor Diarmaid MacCulloch describes her as possessing "a kindly attitude towards radical spirits and a brusque contempt for male intolerance".[1] Forthright Catherine certainly was, but her assertiveness came from her love for God and God's people. From childhood she had been a devout student of Scripture and by 1522 she had accepted Luther's basic teaching. By then she was in her mid-twenties and, unusually for those days, had shown no interest in matrimony. Had she not embraced the new theology, Catherine would probably have been one of the "stars" of the Catholic mystical tradition. Like Catherine of Siena or Teresa of Avila, she was possessed by the reality of the love of God but, whereas those earlier contemplatives had taken erotic love as their image of the mystical union of Christ and the believer, for Catherine Zell it was the experience of motherhood that brought her close to the heart of God. Not for her the suppressed sexuality of the chaste virgin; the love of God, she wrote, was something that "a woman who has never had a child, never experienced or felt the pain of birth and the love of feeding a nursling cannot understand". "Jesus Christ is the true mother," she averred.[2] She had two children of her own but both died in infancy. Thereafter, all members of God's family, especially those who were suffering, became her children. Indeed, the "title" she applied to herself was "church mother".

Like a battling matriarch, she vigorously defended her right to speak on behalf of her spiritual charges. When the bishop enjoined her to obey St Paul's injunction to be silent, she responded:

I would remind you of the word of this same apostle that in Christ there is no longer male nor female and of the prophecy of Joel: "I will pour forth my spirit upon all flesh and your sons and your daughters *will prophesy."* I do not pretend to be John the Baptist *rebuking the Pharisees. I do not claim to be Nathan upbraiding David, I aspire only to be Balaam's ass, castigating his master.*[3]

She was equally forthright in defending clerical marriage; so much so that the bishop complained to the town council of her "abusive" language. Strasbourg was certainly in need of such women in the 1520s and 1530s. Drawn by its reputation for toleration, refugees flocked into the city. Some were reformists fleeing Catholic persecution. Some were men, women, and children forced from their homes by the Peasants' War. But there were also people escaping from discord among the emerging Protestant groups. Luther's rebellion had given permission to other theologians – professional and amateur – to develop their own ideas about major Christian doctrines. At least, that is what many independent preachers believed. The "back-to-the-Bible" principle involved the discarding of fifteen hundred years of authoritative church teaching and encouraged a variety of religious radicalisms. Differences between the major groupings in Germany and Switzerland were neither numerous nor, judged by modern standards, fundamental. Leaders such as Johannes Oecolampadius at Basel and Huldrych Zwingli at Zurich differed seriously from Luther only on the nature of Christ's presence in the Mass (or Eucharist or Supper of the Lord). But there were others in those heady days of intellectual freedom who went much further. Often lumped together as Anabaptists, these extremists represented a wide variety of unorthodox views and were as much anathema to the main Protestant leaders as they were to the Catholic hierarchy (see below). Thus, within a decade of Luther's challenge of papal practices in 1517, the Reformation had fragmented. The movement's more moderate leaders regarded this as a major scandal and did their utmost to close the cracks appearing in the evangelical world. The clergy of Strasbourg saw themselves as having an eirenic mission. In 1529 they attended a meeting at Marburg with their German and Swiss counterparts, prepared to consider compromises in the interests of unity, but Luther was adamant and the conference broke up without achieving anything.

If they could not bring their separated brothers to agreement, the Strasbourgers could, at least, practise charity towards them. The city gates were open, not only to refugees from conflict but also to scholars of all persuasions seeking truth and brotherhood. Strasbourg really was, to use a cliché, a theological melting pot. We have the disadvantage of looking back on these Protestant infancy years from the viewpoint of the divisions which later became entrenched, but the situation at the time was much more fluid. "Lutheranism", "Zwinglianism", "Calvinism", "Anabaptism", "Humanism", and "radicalism" had not emerged as fixed doctrinal systems, each claiming to define immutable truth. For those few years Christian thinkers were trying to frame a theology and an ecclesiology freed from papal control. Indeed, there were many Catholic scholars who accepted the need for reform and were open to change. Strasbourg was a nursery where many open-minded Christians came together. It was in this atmosphere that Catherine Zell played an important part.

> *We ought to exercise and practise towards each other … the office*
> *of care and love … the whole Scripture teaches us to love and serve*
> *our neighbours as the members of one body and help each other bear*
> *evil …* [4]

It was in this spirit that Catherine opened her home to all who were in need of refuge, regardless of their opinions. She was in full accord with her husband in placing spiritual fellowship above theological precision. Matthew declared, "Anyone who acknowledges Christ as the true Son of God and the sole Saviour of mankind is welcome at my board."[5] The Zells' parsonage house was frequently filled with visitors, whether delegates from other churches or persecuted souls totally dependent on their charity. When Matthew travelled to meetings with other reformist church leaders it was not unusual for his wife to accompany him. She did not take part in their scholarly debates but she certainly availed herself of the opportunity to engage in private conversation with the leading theologians of the day and to extend her knowledge.

This degree of involvement by a "mere woman" was not always well received. Authority figures were in a quandary. They and their forefathers back to who knew when had been brought up in a male-dominated society. The doctors of the church had long since bolstered the status quo with doctrines that gave divine sanction to the subservience of the daughters of Eve. Seldom had they been called upon to make a serious effort to challenge women like Catherine Zell who were enlarging their status and extending their influence beyond the confines of their domestic calling. But now, active wives whose evangelical credentials were unimpeachable were taking troublesome initiatives. What was worse was that they were defending their "interference" by appeal to holy writ:

> *Did Jesus only say, "Go preach my Gospel to wise lords and grand doctors?" Did he not say, "to all?" Do we have two gospels, one for men and the other for women? … we ought not, any more than men, hide and bury within the earth that which God has … revealed to us women.*[6]

So wrote Marie Dentière (c. 1495–1561), another early Protestant matriarch of the pattern with which we are now becoming familiar. She was a former abbess who had become convinced by

Luther's writing, left her convent, and married a French pastor, with whom she established a joint ministry in Geneva. This was revolutionary stuff, and if it scandalized traditionalists, it also began to trouble the male leaders of reform. When their own spouses began quoting Scripture against them, matters were clearly getting out of hand.

Just how far out of hand, Catherine Zell was soon demonstrating. With impunity she broke the rules – not only the unspoken conventions, but also the written codes established by decree. For one thing, her charity was wide enough to embrace men condemned unanimously as heretics by all the Strasbourg clergy. Among her one-time house guests was Caspar Schwenkfeld, a radical mystic whose dependence upon the inner testimony of the Holy Spirit led him to disregard not just the authority of popes, councils, and preachers but also that of the Bible. Catherine's friendship with this "fanatic" angered the Strasbourg establishment. But she was unapologetic in her determination to show love and compassion to all in need. When one of Schwenkfeld's disciples died and was refused a Christian burial, Catherine rose from her sickbed and personally presided over the ceremony.

When women like Catherine struck out on their own in defiance of their religious networks, they claimed the freedom which was an aspect of their spiritual inheritance. "We must obey God rather than men" is a claim that we not infrequently encounter in their letters and spoken testimony. Some felt absolved from meek obedience even to their spouses. One such was Anne Locke (1530–c.1590). She came from impeccable Protestant stock in the City of London. Her father, Stephen Vaughan, had been a close associate of Thomas Cromwell and a supporter of William Tyndale when the translator was in Antwerp, working on the English New Testament. Her mother had an honoured place in the household of Queen Anne Boleyn. Anne's parents made a suitable and agreeable marriage for her with Henry Locke, a member of the Mercers' Company and a man who shared their parents' Protestant convictions. All was well until Catholic Mary Tudor came to the throne. Like Mistress Zell, Anne played hostess and protectoress to several radical activists. But that was a dangerous thing to do and Anne soon found herself among the "marked" people in whom the regime was taking a close interest. Like scores of other evangelicals, Anne decided to seek refuge in one of the continental Protestant cities. In 1557, she set off for Geneva with her two small children but *without her husband*.

We may speculate about this desertion. It certainly did not indicate permanent estrangement. Within the year, as soon as Queen Mary had been replaced by her mildly Protestant half-sister, Anne returned to her home in Cheapside. It may be that her extreme opinions were attracting dangerous attention from the authorities and that her departure "until the times do alter" was a wise move, which would allow her more moderate husband to continue his business without the unwelcome attention of the bishop's men. However, that explanation takes no account of a third party who was involved in the Lockes' lives. One of the refugees who had stayed in their home in 1552–53 was none other than the Scottish firebrand John Knox. He had made a deep impression on Anne and it was in response to his invitation that she decamped to Geneva. Nowadays, such a triangular relationship would almost inevitably raise suggestions of sexual impropriety, but the mid-sixteenth century was a different world. It was the norm for ladies of a religious "bent" to have confessors and spiritual directors, who were, of course, male. It was quite natural for those who espoused the reform to seek instruction and guidance from evangelical preachers, just as it was for their Catholic neighbours to look to their priests for absolution. And just as there had always been priests who had attracted considerable followings of female devotees, so the new faith produced celebrities popular with the ladies. None was more popular than John Knox.

Knox's faith was masculine and muscular. He preached with certainty and forthrightness, untinged by doubt or hesitation. He had an impressive personal story to tell of persecution at the hands of French Catholics, who had worked him almost to death in the naval galleys. Added to all this, he was physically strong and an impressive wielder of a two-handed sword. In 1556, he had accepted a post as minister of one of the Genevan churches and was an eager disciple of John Calvin. He was soon writing to friends in England and Scotland extolling the virtues of what he described as "the most perfect school of Christ that ever was". Whatever her motivations, Anne Locke was one of those who decided to leave her home in order to experience the spiritual delights of this godly commonwealth.

Clearly the reality did not disappoint her. The Geneva polity based on a close partnership of magistrates and Christian ministers made a lasting impression on Anne; no other system would ever bear comparison for her. Having drunk deeply of the pure milk of Calvinism, she became an active member of the Puritan community who wished to see the Anglican church replaced by one based on the Genevan pattern. In London her house was, once again, open to members of the more radical Protestant community. Knox had by now returned to Scotland to lead the Reformation north of the border and establish a Presbyterian form of church government. He and his erstwhile disciple never met again but they did keep up a correspondence, which reveals the high regard Knox had for his old friend. As part of her contribution to the radicalization of the English church, Anne made translations of some of Calvin's sermons. Another small volume, a paraphrase of Psalm 51, still exists in the British Library, with a touching inscription by Anne to her husband.

On Henry Locke's death in 1571, Anne was left a wealthy widow in her mid-thirties. As such she would not have lacked for suitors. The one she favoured was probably the nearest she could find to her ideal, John Knox. Edward Dering was the rector of Pluckley in Kent but was more often to be found in London and at the royal court, where he had a reputation as a formidable preacher and a forthright opponent of the Anglican system. Indeed, his career took a pronounced turn for the worse when, in a sermon before the queen, he inveighed against rule by bishops. This was shortly before his marriage to Anne and is a clear indication of her identification with religious opinions that were decidedly non-PC. Dering was younger than his bride, possibly by as much as ten years, and, like Knox, he was also popular with devout ladies. He had many admirers in the city and at court – though Queen Elizabeth was, clearly, not among them. Her aversion to Puritans ran deep and, in 1573, she issued proclamations aimed at silencing forthright preachers. The list included Dering, and no amount of intercession by Anne's friends at court could help him. It seems that Anne was also on the queen's blacklist but Dering assured a friend that, if she were to be examined, "God hath made her rich in grace and knowledge to give account of her doing".[7] Sadly, Anne was destined to be widowed a second time. Edward Dering died of tuberculosis in 1576.

It may have been prudence that prompted Anne to put some distance between herself and London. She retired to Exeter and there married one of the leading citizens of the city, Richard Prowse, a wealthy draper who represented Exeter in parliament and was three times mayor. It is no surprise that Anne's third husband was "of the faith" and associated with prominent Protestant West Country families such as the Carews and the Peryams. Anne maintained from a distance her contacts with friends at the centre of national life and, as we shall see (see below), she employed her relative seclusion in writing for the edification of her brethren.

Anne enjoyed the patronage of women in the inner circle of Queen Elizabeth. Among them was one of the most colourful personalities of the English Reformation, Catherine Bertie, Dowager Duchess of Suffolk (1519–1580). This feisty lady was half-Spanish and may have inherited a certain haughtiness from her mother, a lady-in-waiting to Catherine of Aragon. At the age of sixteen (1536), she was married to Henry VIII's close friend, Charles Brandon, Duke of Suffolk. She was thus a person of consequence at the royal court and could get away with behaviour that, for other women, would have meant banishment. Having come to embrace the reformed faith, she became an extremely active member of an evangelical network which embraced members of the court, publishers of Protestant propaganda, and preachers in London, Suffolk, and the East Midlands, where she was a major landowner. The most prolific printer and publisher of Protestant books and tracts during the latter days of Henry VIII and the reign of Edward VI was John Day, whose premises were close by the duchess's town house. Several books from his press carry plates displaying her coat of arms. Her financial assistance and the use of her name both boosted sales.[8] Among the preachers who enjoyed her support, her favourite was Hugh Latimer, whom she spoke of as her spiritual "father".

Catherine was lively and held strong opinions, and rarely hesitated to express them. This meant that she attracted enemies as easily as she did friends. One of her own supporters commented how unfortunate it was "that so goodly a wit waiteth upon so forward a will".[9] The main victim of her sharp tongue was Bishop Gardiner, the king's most influential Catholic councillor. One story often told of her is that she kept a pet dog and called him Gardiner. Her taunts undoubtedly stung him but he was powerless to prevent them – for the time being. But the bishop was not the sort of man to swallow humiliation, and he had a long memory. The Duke of Suffolk died in 1545 and Catherine, unusually for the time, chose to remain a widow for seven years. She had inherited considerable wealth from her father and her husband and did not lack for suitors. Her eventual selection of a new spouse raised several eyebrows. She married a member of her own household staff.

It was a love match and, perhaps, it should not have surprised any who knew her well. Earlier, Edward Seymour, Duke of Somerset, at that time the most powerful man in England, had proposed a marriage between his infant daughter and one of Catherine's young sons. This arrangement – quite normal at the time – Catherine refused to countenance. "I cannot tell what more unkindness one of us might show … than to bring our children into so miserable an estate not to choose by their own likings."[10] Catherine had long since realized that the major decisions of life should not be made with regard only to material considerations. Religion must play an important part, and it did so in the case of her second marriage. Richard Bertie was a man of modest family who had entered the service of the duchess and who, in his mid-thirties, was now her master of the horse. He was also described as "earnest in religion". Within months of the couple's nuptials Catholic Mary Tudor was on the throne. Even more ominously, Bishop Stephen Gardiner was the queen's right-hand man. Within months he set about settling old scores. He summoned Bertie and demanded that he bring his wife to a "true" understanding of the Mass. It was something of an embarrassment that a lady of Spanish blood (like the queen herself) should be such a notorious Protestant at a time when Mary Tudor was about to marry the King of Spain. Bertie temporized. Obtaining permission to travel abroad on business, he used the time to plan his escape to the continent with his wife.

"Escape" might be a romantic way of describing their departure. When John Foxe was writing his martyrology, he made use of an account by Richard Bertie of the dangers, wanderings, and hardships experienced by himself and his wife. It was a colourful adventure story, consisting of disguisings, pursuits, and close shaves. Catherine made her "getaway" attended by a small entourage which can hardly have failed to be conspicuous, however, and Mary's court must have been glad to see the back of her. Putting such a prominent lady on trial would have been an embarrassment and, after her flight, the regime was able to confiscate the dowager duchess's considerable landed wealth. So the Berties' removal to the continent created a win–win situation for all concerned. That is not to say that the following years were not hard for the fugitives. Catherine was already pregnant when they arrived in the Low Countries. At Wesel she gave birth to a son. But they were unable to settle there. Everywhere in religion-torn Europe they encountered sometimes hospitality but more often suspicion and harassment. They moved eastward by stages: Strasbourg, Frankfurt, Weinheim, until eventually finding a welcome from King Sigismund Augustus in distant Poland. As well as the hardships and the uncertainties of constant travel, the refugees must have been often bemused by the atmosphere among fellow émigrés in the various cities through which they passed. For example, the contrast between eirenic Strasbourg and faction-torn Frankfurt could hardly have been greater. In the latter city the English exiles were divided over liturgy and church order. Some were content to use the revised Prayer Book drawn up during the reign of Edward VI but others regarded it as a compromise with popish ceremonies. It was clear that, if and when the Protestant fugitives returned to England, they would take their quarrels with them.

As for the Berties, the doctrinal wranglings they had encountered affected their religious convictions. They would not find *ecclesia anglicana* entirely to their liking. Catherine wasted no time in taking William Cecil, the queen's first minister, to task. Before her party had even left Poland she wrote to deplore the news of half-hearted reform that had reached her. As Elijah had demanded to know of the people of Israel faced with the claims of Baal and the God of their fathers, so Catherine challenged Cecil: "How long halt ye between two opinions?" She had the exile's contempt for those who, like Cecil, had stayed at home and temporized. They had worn their faith in a slovenly fashion, like ill-fitting hose, and "it is to be feared men have so long worn the Gospel slopewise that they will not gladly have it again straight to their legs".[11] She urged the minister to have nothing to do with either Rome or Wittenberg but to follow the plain rule of Christ. Exactly what she meant by that became clear over the ensuing years. Catherine became the "mother superior" to the more extreme Puritans. When her lands were returned to her she had considerable patronage to bestow and preachers enjoying her protection were thorns in the side of bishops trying to enforce the Elizabethan settlement (see below). The London church of Holy Trinity Minories was a particular problem for the establishment. It actually lay just outside the eastern wall and was part of the Liberties of the Tower of London. As such it was independent of the bishop. The dowager duchess owned a property in the parish and she was very much the dominant figure in the locality. It is no surprise to learn that Holy Trinity became a Puritan "cathedral" where extremist preachers regularly occupied the pulpit, preaching to supporters who came from all over the capital and beyond.

Catherine Zell, Anne Locke, and Catherine Bertie were all examples of a breed of women who embraced their conventional domestic and social roles and sought through them to disseminate their religious convictions. Without doubt, they were the dominant personalities in their households. That did not mean that they "wore the trousers"; simply that their zeal attracted attention and that their husbands were content to support them in their endeavours.

As the sixteenth century drew towards its close, the phenomenon of the educated and active Protestant woman was no longer a novelty. That did not mean that such ladies were universally accepted. They could be resented even within their own families, as the case of formidable Anne Bacon, "the Ghost of Gray's Inn", indicates. Anne was born around 1528 into an awesomely brainy family, the Cookes. Sir Anthony Cooke was a natural scholar to whom it would not be inappropriate to ascribe the word "genius". Before he entered his teens he had mastered the classics, history, and mathematics. By the time Edward VI came to the throne Cooke was already a member of a humanist/evangelical set that included such leading intellectuals as John Cheke and Roger Ascham. Like them, he was appointed as a teacher to the young king's household. His own children – four sons and five daughters – were all educated to the highest standard pertaining in Tudor England and were destined through their political and social connections to play leading roles in the life of the nation. Two of the girls were married to men who would be political leaders during the reign of Elizabeth. Mildred was the wife of William Cecil (later Lord Burghley) and Anne's husband was Nicholas Bacon, Lord Keeper of the Great Seal.

Anne was taught Latin, Greek, Hebrew, French, and Italian, and by the age of twenty had gone into print with the translation of a book of sermons by the Italian Protestant Bernardino Ochino, who had found refuge in England. In 1562, John Jewel, Bishop of Salisbury, wrote *Apologia Ecclesias Anglicanae* as a defence of the Elizabethan Settlement against Catholic critics. The scholar who translated this into English two years later was Anne Bacon. Yet, despite this defence of the official religion, she was decidedly on the Puritan wing of the church and maintained a vigorous correspondence with clergy and politicians in her determination to ensure the purity of Anglican doctrine and practice. She argued with erudition, frequently illustrating her points from ancient authors and citing them in the original Greek or Latin. If anyone protested about "a mere woman" venturing into the hurly-burly of ecclesiastical affairs she had a ready answer: "I think for my long attending in court and a chief councillor's wife, few women in my position are able to be alive to speak and judge of such proceedings and worldly doings of men."[12]

But she did not neglect her duties as wife and mother. She bore two sons, Anthony and Francis, and ensured that their education and upbringing were as rigorous as hers had been. Both boys were sent to Cambridge and then to Gray's Inn. They enjoyed the social life of the legal fraternity whose buildings were situated between London and Westminster, where they could sample the diversions offered by the city and the court. Their only problem lay in the visits and letters of their over-protective mother and her determination to protect them from the fleshpots. In one of his letters home Anthony accused her of having "a sovereign desire to overrule your sons in all things, how little soever you understand either the grounds or the circumstances of [their] proceedings".[13] The teenage brothers and their friends made fun of Lady Bacon and it must have been they who originated a legend that was current in later years. According to this, Anne's ghost could often be seen wandering the courts and chambers of Gray's Inn, wringing her hands and bewailing the loose morals of the students.

While Francis followed a legal and literary career, becoming one of the leading philosophers of the age, Anthony adopted a more rakish lifestyle, mingling with actors, politicians, and spies. He was a disappointment to his mother, but if he did not turn out to be the godly English gentleman she had hoped for,

Anne must bear some of the blame. This domineering woman never let up in her efforts to ensure that her boys followed the paths of righteousness, as she conceived them to be. A series of incidents in 1589 display the fierceness of her own zeal and her determination to direct her elder son (who was by then thirty-one!) in the ways of holiness. Anthony was in France, where, among other things, he collected intelligence for the English government. News of his dissolute life reached his mother but she also learned something far worse: he had set up house with a friend, Thomas Lawson, who was a Catholic. When Lawson was sent to London with information gathered by Anthony, Anne engineered his arrest. Anthony sent another friend, Francis Allen, to intercede with his mother for Lawson's release. When Allen reported on his meeting with Lady Bacon, he described a woman who had flown into a hysterical rage:

> She let not to say that you are a traitor to God and your country; you have undone her; you seek her death … It is in vain to look for Mr Lawson's return, for these are her ladyship's own words: "No, no … I have learned not to employ ill to good."

Lady Bacon, he said, was contemplating asking the queen to recall her son and throw him in prison. Rather than hear that he was consorting with papists, she said that she would receive news that "you had been fairly buried, provided you had died in the Lord".[14] This intractable Puritan matriarch lived well into her eighties, dying, at last, in 1610. By that time any frustration and irritation felt by her sons had faded. Or, perhaps, they had learned to live with her unyielding religious convictions and moral strictures. Whatever the truth of the matter, it is pleasing to note that the great philosopher Sir Francis Bacon requested that on his death (which occurred in 1626) he should be buried beside his mother.

CHAPTER 3

WOMEN IN COMMUNITY

We do not despise marriage. For we know that whoever marries does the right thing ... In the event that we decide to serve God as virgins, truly no intelligent person can hold that against us ... If, however, someone is not so inclined or does not want to join us, we have nothing against that. We, therefore, do not plan to hold back any sister by force or to keep her from her parents ... We also do not want to condemn anyone, but let every man judge for himself; everyone will be judged when we all come before God's judgement. But just as we do not want to force anyone, we also do not want to be forced.[1]

Those words were written by Caritas Pirckheimer, Abbess of the Poor Clares in Nuremberg, in 1525 (see below). They were her response to the city authorities, who, having accepted the Lutheran reform, had ordered the closure of all houses of religion. Her staunch defence of her convent was not the knee-jerk reaction of a closed-minded traditionalist. Caritas was educated in the new liberal Renaissance regimen and her brother, Willibald, was one of the foremost humanist scholars of the age and an early supporter of Luther. However, the siblings, initially at least, did not see eye to eye on the issue of the monasteries. For Caritas (and many other devout women), religious community life was not only a valuable part of the Christian tradition, it was fully in accord with the word of God.

There were good social as well as religious reasons for cloistering women together to lead lives dedicated to prayer. The spiritual impulses and economic necessities which inspired women to separate from the world and live under a common rule of life and worship lie largely outside the scope of this book, but we do need to consider briefly the kind of communities that had developed in the centuries before the Reformation. For many women, especially older ones, communal life was the only alternative to lonely destitution. In epochs riven by disease and civic unrest and in which there was no effective system of state care, many found themselves with no means of subsistence. This group included not only widows and orphans but those who had lost their entire families. Marauding armies frequently carried off the able-bodied men when they raided a village, leaving the less "valuable" occupants (i.e. the women) to fend for themselves. Well-to-do families overburdened with daughters for whom marriage dowries had to be found often resorted to placing some of their excess females in convents where, in return for a generous initial payment, the girls would be cared for in respectable institutions, receive a better-than-average education, and be dedicated to God. Several convents were, in effect, boarding establishments for the daughters of noble houses. Members who rose to be abbesses were on a par with other leaders of polite society, exercising considerable authority over extensive abbatial estates and enjoying status among the social elite. Thus, in many ways female religious orders provided solutions to very real problems and were regarded as essential, not only by those interested in fostering devotion to God. While some inmates welcomed the possibility of escape, the majority must have been alarmed at the prospect of their houses being closed and their entire way of life coming to an end. The religious life was considered to be the purest medium for serving God and, from early times, devout women had asserted that they had as much right as their menfolk to pursue the communal route to holiness. Most orders founded for women were sister houses of existing male establishments. But there were several unattached, semi-monastic communities, especially in the Low Countries. They were spontaneous groups of "beguines", lay women who felt called to pray and study together and to serve their communities, largely by caring for the poor and the sick. These beguinages followed none of the conventional rules of life laid down by such monastic pioneers as Francis and Benedict and they were, not infrequently, regarded with suspicion and hostility by the ecclesiastical authorities.

Like any institution, monastic life could become moribund, more concerned with maintaining a system than with opening up new ways of fulfilling the role prescribed by the founders. But the institution was far from being impervious to reform and, over the centuries, revivalist movements had appeared from time to time which sought to restore vigour to the religious way of life. The Brothers and Sisters of the Common Life were one such movement. Established in the Netherlands and North Germany in the fifteenth century, it consisted of open communities of lay people living according to the *Devotio Moderna*, or "New Devotional System". Members pledged themselves to life in single-sex communities (or, in some cases, family-based groupings), where they espoused a quality and intensity of spiritual experience not conventionally available outside the monastic cloister. One of their number, Thomas à Kempis, gave the movement its most popular manual, *The Imitation of Christ*, which ran through twenty imprints in Germany alone between 1486 and 1500. Sisters worked in the world, meeting the needs of the poor and the sick, but they became particularly devoted to the cause of education. They founded schools and ran student hostels to provide children and teenagers with the basics of literacy, Latin, and mathematics but also to elevate their minds to heavenly realities. One of their pupils at a school in Magdeburg was the young Martin Luther. The principles of the Common Life would influence him later when he presided over the student hostel he established in Wittenberg.

Beyond these again were what we might call the "non-community nuns". These were women attracted to the spiritual disciplines of regular prayer and devotional exercise but who were not in a position to abandon their responsibilities as members of lay society. One striking example was Lady Margaret Beaufort (1443–1509), mother of Henry VII, England's first Tudor king. Although deeply involved in the scheming and intrigue of dynastic politics, her first priority was the service of God. She took a vow of chastity and lived separately from her husband. Her daily routine was organized round the recitation of the monastic offices. She was officially enrolled as a "sister" in several religious houses, and in her own chapel she employed several priests to celebrate Mass almost continuously. Margaret studied devotional works, under the guidance of her confessor, John Fisher, Bishop of Rochester (later beheaded by Margaret's grandson, Henry VIII), and translated into English part of *The Imitation of Christ* and *The Mirror of Gold for the Sinful Soul*, by the Flemish Carthusian mystic Jacobus de Gruytroede. Her philanthropy was legendary. Not only did she exercise charity towards the poor who flocked to her door, she was the age's major patroness of scholars, founding colleges and professorships at both English universities. Her concern was to improve the academic standards of the clergy and encourage good-quality preaching (in her will she left bequests for regular sermons).

In short, it is clear that medieval Catholicism provided various opportunities for women to pursue personal holiness and to serve their neighbours. There remains one more category of traditional feminine piety to be considered. It takes us into the world of Christian mysticism. Throughout the medieval centuries there appeared an almost constant stream of visionaries whose ecstatic utterances, they claimed, were the result of their being under the irresistible power of the Holy Spirit. A remarkable number of these "prophets" were women. Their messages usually involved calling to repentance an ecclesiastical establishment which had become moribund or had stumbled into error. Some were cloistered sisters, some anchorites, and some members of the laity, but all, by their charismatic conviction, attracted large followings. It may be difficult to explain why such bold "rebels" as Hildegard of Bingen, Catherine of Siena, and Bridget of Sweden were tolerated within a male-dominated church (some mystics eventually went too far and suffered the consequences), but they seem to have acted as a safety valve which allowed criticisms to be aired and reform movements to be contained.

As the sixteenth century progressed, dissatisfaction with aspects of church life became more widespread and difficult to contain. One feature of European life which emerged was an increase in the number of female ecstatics. In devout Catholic convents and in no-less-devout Anabaptist assemblies charismatic women appeared, adding their voices to the demand for reform (see below). An alarmed Catholic hierarchy adopted a zero-tolerance policy towards visionary excesses both within and without religious houses. In 1542 Pope Paul III issued the bull *Licet ab initio*, which set up the Holy Office to take charge of the war against heresy in all lands and endowed it with almost unlimited powers. From that time the Vatican mounted a vigorous campaign to seek out and destroy all traces of error in convent life.

One area notably in the grip of reform was North Italy where, among people at all levels of church life, there was

a renewed emphasis on the grace which God sent through faith, together with a consistent urge to reveal the Holy Spirit as the force conveying this grace – so that associates of the movement were soon characterized as Spirituali.[2]

Several of the *Spirituali* thinkers were treading a parallel path to Luther's, though all of them hoped to influence Catholic *lexis* and *praxis* from within. Several of the new initiatives were made possible by influential female patrons. Wealthy ladies, moved by the preaching of ardent priests and itinerant evangelists calling for conversion – complete reorientation of life for the service of God – gave money, land or buildings to groups wishing to establish convents as centres of their religious life and bases for outreach (see below). Prominent among these benefactors was Countess Ludovica Torelli, a childless widow possessed of extensive property bordering the River Po between Parma and Mantua. Blessed with wealth, ease, and leisure, Ludovica could have enjoyed to the full the life of the idle rich but, as she later wrote, "I lived as lost, and cried out to my love, Jesus Christ: I am not one of yours."[3] Her ardent spiritual quest led to her conversion, after which she devoted her entire fortune to religious reform. The result was the Order of San Paolo Converso, a threefold foundation for monks (Barnabites), nuns (Angelics), and lay couples (Paulines). The headquarters of the new order was established in Milan in 1535.

Among its first members were the sisters Battista and Paola Antonia (1508–1555) Negri. Paola was in her late twenties but already had a reputation as a mystic and ecstatic. She was a strong-willed charismatic, the sort of person who sweeps others along on the tide of her own convictions. Although Battista became the prioress of the Angelics, her sister was regarded as the real leader. "Christ lives in her, works miracles through her and on her has founded and rested this whole edifice,"[4] so enthused one of her devotees. But what was really remarkable about Paola Negri was not her primacy among the Angelics but her dominance over all members of the order – male, as well as female. They called her their "divine mother" and looked to her to confirm or reject all decisions. Backed to the hilt by the foundress, Countess Torelli, Paola established a unique matriarchy that survived for almost fifteen years.

She had, by the mid-1540s, encroached extensively on both religious and social conventions and was already attracting the attention of the hierarchy. But it was only when she took control of the sacramental life of the community that alarm bells rang loudly in high places. She determined what priests should be appointed, how they should perform their duties, and, crucially, when they should say Mass and who should be excluded from the rite as punishment. There was even a rumour (never confirmed) that she had committed the unforgivable sin of presiding over the sacramental service herself.

The conflict between rigid orthodoxy and religious fervour was not new. There had always been convents which were spiritual hothouses, largely unsupervised by the bishops, where luxuriant mysticism and unconventional expressions of piety could flourish. Moreover, because visionaries, miracle workers, and charismatic preachers tended to be popular with the people, they were even more difficult to control. But now something clearly had to be done and the Vatican went onto the offensive.

Matters came to a head in 1551, not in Milan but in Venice, where Paola and some of her colleagues had gone to work in a hospital. The city fathers were, as they said, scandalized by the irregularities among the Paulines: "The priests kneel down before this mother teacher, who grants and refuses them permission to celebrate and teaches and interprets Scripture."[5] Paola and all her colleagues were expelled from Venetian territory. When spokesmen from Milan went to Rome to protest about the ban, they found themselves in the Inquisitions prison, being forced to defend the entire ethos of their order.

In the confrontation between the Holy Office and the Pauline leadership neither side was prepared to yield. Countess Torelli stood staunchly by the divine mother. The Roman hierarchy demanded sweeping reforms and threatened to disband the order. It was the Barnabites who buckled first. Under mounting pressure, the brothers who had claimed that Paola was a mouthpiece of God now conceded, "She is a woman and may be deceived." The pope's decision when it came in June 1552 was, so his holiness claimed, merciful. The deluded woman was to be moved to another convent and denied all contact with the outside world. Paola made a bid to escape but this failed and she was confined within the walls of Santa Chiara, a nunnery of the Poor Clares in Milan. There, less than three years later, she died.

We can only guess what her spiritual agonies may have been in her last days. Had she been condemned to burn as a heretic she might have found that easier to bear. Martyrdom would have ennobled her death. Had she been challenged to recant her errors she could (probably would) have held fast to her convictions. Instead, she was left to long months of self-examination and doubt, without the comfort of friends who still believed in her. She must have asked herself the questions that history continues to ask: "Were her visions from God or the results of an overactive imagination? Did her spiritual leadership of her order stem from divine authority or her own pride?"

It is not difficult to understand the concern caused by such strong-willed women – either deluded and stubborn or saintly and staunchly faithful, according to one's point of view. Faced with such fiery conviction, it was impossible to be neutral. Either you believed the utterances of a prophetess, in which case doubt was a sin against the Holy Spirit, or you dismissed them as demonic delusions. If the visionary had a large following, that, in itself, could make it difficult to denounce her. Even Henry VIII hesitated when the Nun of Kent challenged his attempt to have his marriage to Catherine of Aragon annulled.

Elizabeth Barton, the Nun or Holy Maid of Kent, was a young serving woman who, in 1525, suffered a serious illness during which she experienced a mental state in which she witnessed "wondrous things done in other places while she was neither herself present nor yet heard no report thereof". This sounds very much like what we would now call an "out-of-body experience". She was "miraculously" cured, and thereafter began to experience trance-like states and to receive messages, which she passed on to her growing band of admirers. Archbishop Warham of Canterbury had her examined by a special commission, which pronounced her prophecies to be genuine. Now she was placed in a nunnery and became a major attraction. Increasingly, her prophecies took on a polemical character. She denounced the "heretics" who were disturbing the church and called for strict adherence to Catholic doctrine. The major cause célèbre of the day was Henry VIII's seeking the dissolution of his marriage to Catherine of Aragon in order to marry Anne Boleyn. This was widely unpopular, and Elizabeth became the most strident opponent of the king's plans. In this she was encouraged and, in all probability, mentored by a group of clergy who were using her as a front in what was becoming a dangerous political game. Becoming ever bolder, by 1531 the Holy Maid of Kent was forecasting fearful divine judgment against the king if he did not put away his mistress and return to his wife.

The fact that Henry VIII did not move swiftly to deal with this seditious coven says much about the hold a prophetess like

Elizabeth could exercise over people at all levels of society. Henry had no intention of abandoning his matrimonial plans but he was very religious and was loath to take drastic action against a devout Catholic woman (and one whose following was now numbered in thousands). The next year Elizabeth confronted her sovereign personally when he was visiting Canterbury. She warned him that if he persisted with his designs of marrying Anne Boleyn he would die within six months and go straight to hell. Still the king took no action. What he did do was set his chief minister, Thomas Cromwell, to discredit Elizabeth. A whispering campaign was launched which accused her of sexual improprieties with priests and of faking her prophecies. Subtle innuendo was more effective than a public trial. Some of the Maid's main supporters were bullied into deserting her as doubts about her morals and her sanity spread. By 1533 Henry was not only married to his new wife and in good health, he was the father of a newborn daughter. He had defied the Maid's prophecies and emerged triumphant. Clearly, God was on his side, not hers. It was time to drive the point home. Elizabeth and her coteries were arrested and thrown into the Tower. There, probably under torture, she confessed to fabricating her divine revelations. She and six others were pronounced guilty of treason and hanged. Elizabeth's head was subsequently displayed atop a pole on London Bridge – the only woman ever to have achieved this mark of notoriety.

Elizabeth Barton and Paola Negri emerged from the Catholic mystical tradition but the majority of "spiritual" women who gained prominence belonged to a very different socio-religious grouping. The radicals sprang up from the illiterate underclass. Fired by Reformation fervour but unable to feed the flames with profound biblical exposition, they sought the oxygen of ecstatic spiritual experience. They shared with mainstream Protestants a commitment to the principle of salvation by grace through faith, but whereas Luther and other evangelical leaders wished to proceed with measured tread, challenging only existing institutions which were in defiance of the will of God as revealed in Scripture, these groups were impatient for root-and-branch change. They easily overlapped with social and political revolutionaries, eager to assail the bastion of church and state. In the eyes of the authorities they were violent rebels – anticlerical, anti-government preachers of apocalyptic mayhem who sought to establish the "rule of the saints". This was why Luther emphatically disassociated himself from them.

The majority, however, concentrated their endeavours on purely religious change. The main centres of activity were Switzerland, Southern Germany/Austria, North Germany, and the Low Countries. They never constituted a movement and operated on the networking principle (some groups were actually mutually hostile). It was their enemies who gave them the generic term "Anabaptist" because the practice all these radicals shared was an insistence on second baptism (or believers' baptism) as a prerequisite of membership. They rejected infant baptism along with ordination and other Catholic sacraments. They took Luther's "priesthood of all believers" to its logical conclusion, allowing freedom to every believer "anointed" by the Holy Spirit to exercise his or her spiritual gifts. They were Bible-based but insisted that the written word always needed to be interpreted by the Spirit (and certainly not by learned theologians). Their exegesis frequently challenged current conventions. For example, some believed that the Bible sanctioned Anabaptist women to leave unbelieving husbands and abandon their families.

Prophecy was particularly important to Anabaptists, placing their confidence, as they did, in the guidance and intervention of the Holy Spirit. They urged all believers to be open to the reception of divine messages and to proclaim them boldly. This freedom in the Spirit applied equally to men and women.

Lienhard Jost, a butcher of Strasbourg, was a prophet. In 1524 he suffered a brief spell in prison, though on what charge is not known. Even in tolerant Strasbourg radicals like Jost were not popular, and the city authorities refused to allow Anabaptists a building for worship. Jost was not abashed by any sign of disfavour. Nor was his wife, Ursula (fl.1520–30); as she later recorded: "After my husband and spouse was released from custody ... he and I together prayed earnestly and diligently to God, the almighty merciful Father, that he would let me also see the wondrous deeds of his hand."[6]

Their prayers were, they believed, affirmatively answered. Over the next few months, when large tracts of the country were convulsed by the Peasants' War, Ursula proclaimed a number of divine revelations. They were all apocalyptic in character, foretelling the dire punishments about to be unleashed by a powerful God whose patience with disobedient humanity was coming to an end. Their effect was dramatic and was a strong influence on the growth of Anabaptism within the city. It is estimated that by 1530 around 10 per cent of the Strasbourg population belonged to the radical wing of the Reformation. That was the year in which seventy-seven of her prophecies were published. *Prophetic Visions and Revelations of the Workings of God in these Last Days, which Were Revealed through the Holy Spirit from 1524 until 1530* was taken up and used by Melchior Hoffman, a much-travelled Anabaptist missionary who identified himself as Elijah, come to establish God's kingdom on earth, with Strasbourg as the new Jerusalem. He was arrested in 1533 and spent his remaining years in prison. Ursula, it seems, was already dead, for there is no record of her after 1530.

She was not the only prophetess to appear on the radical fringe, particularly among Anabaptist groups established throughout the Netherlands and North Germany. Why women should achieve an authoritative role in male-dominated churches is an interesting question. Their claim to direct contact with God neatly bypassed the hierarchy of priests, bishops, and doctors of the church. Jesus himself had taught that the Holy Spirit's activity was like a powerful but invisible wind, unpredictable. Claims of direct spiritual activity made by or on behalf of semi-educated women could not be automatically dismissed and were even more credible at such a time of violent upheaval as the 1520s and 1530s. After the first shockwave of the Reformation was spent, however, social norms reasserted themselves in Protestant communities, just as they did in the Catholic world. There were very few prophetesses after the mid-century.

It has been argued by feminist historians, with a fair degree of justification, that, far from freeing women from a system which restricted their religious activity, the Protestant Reformation actually imposed more stringent restraints. They were denied a life of contemplation in communion with like-minded women and virtually forced into matrimony. This brings us back to the closure of religious houses and the activities of women who resisted it.

The vow of chastity was arduous, particularly for younger women, and Catherine von Bora was typical of many who were happy to abandon it. For some it was as simple as that, but others, because they had the education and the leisure to keep abreast of the latest developments in theology, sought release from their convents on religious grounds. However, there were not a few who saw no contradiction in embracing the Reformation yet continuing their conventual life. Caritas Pirckheimer was eager to assure the Nuremberg authorities that she and her sisters were committed to the vernacular Scriptures and dependence on divine grace rather than good works:

We can say to your honours in truth that we read and use the Old and New Testament in German and in Latin daily, and that as far

as possible we attempt to understand it correctly ... We also know
that we should not attribute our own good works to ourselves, but if
something good happens through us, it is not our work, but God's.[7]

Barbara Pirckheimer (1466–1532) and her younger brother,
Willibald (1470–1530), were members of one of Nuremberg's
wealthiest families. Both received a rich humanist education and
Willibald, after studying in Paris, returned to his home town to
take a prominent place on the council. By this time his sister had
joined the Poor Clares, taking the name "Caritas". By the time
the Reformation storm broke, the two Pirckheimers were senior
and respected members of Nuremberg society. Willibald, the
honest scholar, weighed up the arguments presented by Catholic
and Protestant disputants and concluded that the continuance
of monasticism could not be justified. He failed to convince his
sibling, who refused to release any of her sisters. Their vows,
she said, had been made to God and it was not in her power to
cancel them. Matters came to a head in 1525 when a mob broke
into the convent. Some mothers dragged their daughters away
screaming.

Peace was restored thanks largely to the intervention of
Luther's assistant, Philip Melanchthon. Willibald, shocked by the
violence, elicited his friends' help. The result was a compromise.
No sister would be forced to leave the convent and those wishing
to remain could do so for the rest of their lives. However, they
were forbidden to indulge in Catholic practices such as attending
Mass or auricular confession. No new novices might be accepted
for the convent, which closed when the last inmate died in 1590.
This solution was endorsed by Luther.

Matters did not always end in accommodations that, to some
extent, brought a measure of closure to the grief and angst
experienced by women whose devotion and way of life were
threatened. In Augsburg, for example, eight communities were

allowed to continue in 1534 while all others were disbanded, but, three years later, the houses which had been reprieved were also ordered to close. When the Benedictine or Dominican nuns refused to budge, they had Protestant abbesses imposed upon them. That was not the end of the affair. After a military reverse in 1547 the religious houses were reopened and Catholic practices restored. Such to-ing and fro-ing was commonplace as the Protestant tide ebbed and flowed. Behind all these stories there lie untold tales of divided families, disrupted lives, and frustrated devotion. One of the Augsburg nuns was Catherine Rem. She was strongly urged by her zealous brother, Bernhardt, to leave the sisterhood of Antichrist. In reply she wrote,

> *God will fortify us because we praise and favour him ... We regard you as one of the false prophets that Jesus warned us against in the holy gospels when he said, "Guard yourselves against prophets who come in the form of sheep and are ravening wolves"... we place our hope in God. He is the true lord and rewarder of all things. Him do we serve more willingly in the convent than in the world, with the grace and help of God. You don't have to worry at all about our bodies and souls. You don't have to go to heaven or hell for us. God Almighty will judge all of us at the Last Judgement, according to his justice ... Therefore think about yourself, that you will become and be a good Christian ...[8]*

But all was not *Stürm und Drang* among the nunneries which found themselves in Protestant lands. The convent of Quedlinburg, between Leipzig and Hanover, was one of the richest in Germany. It was founded as a Benedictine house for the daughters of noble houses and was richly endowed. Its abbess commanded extensive estates and enjoyed the title "Imperial Princess". The lady who held that position in the 1520s and 1530s as the Reformation got under way was Anna von Stolberg-Wernigerode (1504–1574).

She became an early convert to Lutheranism but would not declare her allegiance out of deference to the local ruler, Duke George of Saxony, staunch enemy of Luther and cousin of Luther's patron, Frederick the Wise. In 1539, George died and was succeeded by his Protestant brother, Henry IV. Now, Anna lost no time in completely changing the regimen of the abbey. Out went most of the ancient rituals.

Why was she not asked to close the nunnery? The answer has to be that it was too powerful, too influential, and too rich. Anna used her position to install Lutheran pastors in all the churches under her control (not to mention two male monasteries which acknowledged her as temporal overlord). She completely overhauled religious life in the territories under her sway and obliged all priests to sign up to the Lutheran Augsburg Confession. One of her more radical innovations was the founding of a school for both boys and girls.

Quedlinburg Abbey may be considered as a model followed by several religious houses in Germany. Their survival acts as a corrective to any assumption that Luther and his followers were totally opposed to all religious houses. Many of them were so firmly stitched into the fabric of society that tearing them out would have actually hindered the work of reform. Important work could be and was found for these communities of holy women. As well as traditional roles such as running hospitals and almshouses, Protestant convents played an increasing role in education. Many survived well into the nineteenth century, enabling talented and visionary women to exercise, through community living, a greater degree of social and moral influence than their married friends and relatives could aspire to in a male-dominated world.

CHAPTER 4

WOMEN IN POWER

Sixteenth-century society was highly stratified. From emperor and pope down to the meanest, landless peasant, every person had his/her allotted place and was enjoined to keep to it. Those in authority were always nervous about social mobility and any sign of discontent among the lower orders, which was why the Peasants' War was suppressed so violently (at Luther's urging). Kings, dukes, regional governors, and city councillors all exercised and jealously guarded real power – each to his own degree.

In this grand – and divinely ordained – scheme, women, as we have seen, played a subordinate role to men. And yet, and yet, matters were not as clear-cut as that might suggest. Another principle was at work, which often ran counter to that governing relations between the sexes.

This was the dynastic principle. All families in power were determined to remain in power. But what happened if there were no adult males to take up the reins of royal or aristocratic rule? The only answer was – much though it went against the grain – that women had to fill in the gaps. Even in France, where, according to the Salic Law, no woman was permitted to exercise kingly authority, the preservation of the House of Valois demanded that, for many years, the queen mother controlled the government on behalf of her underage sons. In England and Scotland the ruling dynasties simply ran out of princes of the blood royal. The problem of the Holy Roman Empire was one of sheer size: the emperor could not exercise effective central control of his extensive territories, so had to appoint members of his family to act as governors or regents. Several of these viceroys were women. One of the more remarkable facts about the sixteenth century – and it *is* truly remarkable – is the extent of political power vested in women. And even in some territories where queens and regents were not the titular rulers, remarkable strong-willed wives and mothers exercised behind-the-scenes influence.

All this could not but have an impact on the religious life of Europe. In 1555, after a generation of discord had split the states of the empire into warring Catholic and Lutheran camps, peace was made at Augsburg on the basis of the principle *cuius regio, eius religio*, "the ruler's religion is the religion of the state". One result was that, in several places, female rulers were in a position to advance or retard the Reformation. This, in turn, led to some interesting relationships between rulers of church and state. Reformers wedded to the Pauline doctrine that women's role in the household of faith was one of subservience to their menfolk in all matters of doctrine and authority found themselves having to support, encourage, and submit to female heads of state, who were vital to the spread of evangelical religion. The dilemma this could create is illustrated by the well-known miscalculation of the virulent Calvinist polemicist John Knox. In his *First Blast of the Trumpet against the Monstrous Regiment of Women*, he declared that the Reformation in England and Scotland had stalled because God's proscription of rule by women had been flouted in the coming to power of Mary Tudor and Mary of Guise, south and north of the border respectively.

Unfortunately, Knox's diatribe was published in 1558, only months before Mary Tudor died and was replaced by her half-sister, the Protestant Elizabeth I. Protestant she might be, but she was not prepared to be harangued by fiery Calvinist preachers or to turn a blind eye to Knox's vitriolic prose:

> *I fear not to say, that the day of vengeance, which shall apprehend that horrible monster Jezebel of England [i.e. Mary Tudor], and such as maintain her monstrous cruelty, is already appointed in the counsel of the eternal. And I verily believe that it is so nigh, that she shall not reign so long in tyranny as hitherto she has done, when God shall declare himself to be her enemy, when he shall pour forth contempt upon her according to her cruelty, and shall kindle the hearts of such as sometimes did favour her with deadly hatred against her, that they may execute his judgments. And therefore, let such as assist her take heed what they do, for assuredly her empire and reign is a wall without foundation.[1]*

To the new Queen of England, such language was seditious. Not only did she refuse to have Knox in her realm, but she developed a personal loathing of the unyielding Calvinists called Puritans which coloured her religious policy for years (see below).

But we must return to Luther's relationships with politically influential women. "To the noble and virtuous Frau Dorothea Jörger ... my best and true friend in Christ."[2] So he began a letter to one of his many female fans, the widow of an Austrian imperial official, Wolfgang Jörger, who had for several years administered a region of the Tyrol from his castle at Tollet. He died in 1524 as a loyal son of the Catholic Church but he had, unwittingly, set the Reformation in progress by sending his son Christopher to the Elector Frederick's new university at Wittenberg. The young man fell under Luther's spell and returned home as a zealous advocate of his newfound faith. At his request, Lutheran preachers were sent from Wittenberg. This provoked inevitable conflict with the established authority and self-interest of the clergy and their protectors. After three years the reformed preachers were forced to leave. It was then that Dorothea, Christopher's mother, assumed the role of protector of the small Protestant fellowship, frequently turning to Luther for counsel as to how she could maintain love of the Bible in her family, her household, and the wider community. Dorothea responded to his support with frequent gifts for Luther and the poor of Wittenberg who were dependent on his charity (see below). Their correspondence continued for many years and it was through disciples such as Dorothea that the Lutheran reform took root in many distant lands.

Not all relationships were as amicable. In 1537 Elizabeth (1485–1555), wife of Joachim I, Elector of Brandenburg, invited herself and her suite to visit the Luthers. She stayed, and stayed, and stayed. Not only was her presence a strain on her hosts' resources, her behaviour was domineering and eccentric.

Every day there is some fresh annoyance. She barges into the room and even into the bedroom. I won't say that she is simply crazy, but she is childish. When some money did come from her sons, she gave it away lavishly and even to persons she hates … [3]

If Elizabeth was treading the verges of insanity, it is not very difficult to see why. She had been married at the age of seventeen in 1502 in what was a conventional dynastic arrangement. She bore her husband four children and behaved in every way as a dutiful wife – until the time came when she had to choose between Joachim and Luther.

Her fate was an offshoot of the complex politico-religious controversy which lay at the very heart of the Reformation. In order to buy lucrative ecclesiastical offices for members of his family, Joachim had got heavily into debt. To recoup his outlay he did a deal with the papacy for the hawking of indulgences throughout his territories. It was this activity which drew a protest from a certain monk in Wittenberg. All this, of course, was "politics" and, therefore, nothing to do with Joachim's wife. But her husband's notorious philandering was. The couple became estranged and, unsurprisingly, Elizabeth turned to her family for support. Her brother was Christian II of Denmark and he had become a Lutheran. He sent the reformer's writings and, perhaps, evangelical preachers to his sister.

Maintaining her various roles for the next few years – wife, mother, electress, and sister – was increasingly difficult. In addition her own theological understanding was changing. Not until 1527, and then at a time when Joachim was away from home, did Elizabeth openly declare her conversion to Lutheranism. There followed months of bitter argument in which a publicly embarrassed Joachim tried to force his wife to conform with his religion and she tried to explain to him why she could not, in good conscience, do so. Every confrontation made Elizabeth firmer in her newfound convictions. In the spring of 1528, she left her husband.

There now followed seventeen years of wandering, during which time she became more and more intransigent. Even after her husband's death in 1535 she refused to return home except on her own stringent terms. These were not only that she would be free to worship as she wished, but also that Lutheranism would be the official religion in her domain. During this period of self-imposed exile she moved around the courts and homes of relatives and friends (such as the Luthers). Joachim II, who succeeded his father, converted to Protestantism in 1539 and strongly urged his mother to come home, but she seems to have used her own suffering as a means of pressing the reform in Brandenburg to its ultimate limits. She felt that her son had made unacceptable concessions to his Catholic subjects and she stubbornly refused to be fully reconciled with him until public worship had been purged of every trace of papistry. The elector faced the challenge of winning over his people to the new reformed doctrine and in this he actually had the support of Luther, but for his mother it was "all or nothing". Not until the last year of her life (1545) did she allow herself to be honourably escorted to her son's capital, Berlin.

Much of her story was relived by her daughter, known as Elizabeth of Brunswick (1510–1558). She, too, was a teenage bride in a dynastic marriage. Her husband, Eric I, Duke of Brunswick-Göttingen-Calenberg, was twenty-seven years her senior. The troubled history of her parents forced her to take sides, and she supported her mother. Though a loyal supporter of the emperor and the emperor's religion, Eric tolerated his wife's theological deviation. But, once again, sex entered the equation. Eric had a long-term mistress and when Elizabeth fell ill she convinced herself that the other woman had used witchcraft against her. She demanded that the offender be burned, and Eric had to resort to trickery to save his mistress while convincing his wife that the execution order had been given.

Elizabeth was emerging as a woman as strong-willed and single-minded as her mother. When Duke Eric died in 1540, she was appointed co-regent for her underage son (later Eric II). She wasted no time in organizing a thoroughgoing reform of the duchy. A team of preachers and administrators recommended by Luther was brought in to establish new patterns of worship and oversee the teaching of *sola fidei*-based theology in all churches and religious houses. The duchess personally drafted legislative and administrative documents and visited convents to oversee the implementation of change. Some of her edicts almost had the nature of sermons, with biblical texts providing the basis for moral exhortation.

It goes without saying that Eric II was brought up as a good Lutheran and that he was safely married into a Protestant family. Perhaps it also goes without saying that he disentangled himself from his mother's apron strings at the earliest opportunity. Eric was determined to be his own man and did not want to be seen as ruled by a woman. As the conflict within the empire grew between the Catholic states and the Protestant states (the Schmalkaldic League), he sided with the former and told his mother to stop interfering in politics. He reversed the reform, imprisoned some of the ministers, enforced Catholic ceremonial, and rejected his wife because she would not give up her faith. Elizabeth was distraught: "O Lord God," she wrote,

> to whom have I given birth? Whom have I reared? To deny the
> plain truth is a sin which cannot be forgiven in earth or in heaven.
> To persecute, maltreat and abuse the servants of the Word of God
> is to persecute, maltreat and abuse Christ Jesus our only Saviour,
> mediator and intercessor, who has borne our sins.[4]

Elizabeth had by now remarried. Her husband, Count Poppo XII of Henneberg (a small Thuringian territory between Frankfurt and Erfurt), was a man who shared her faith. With him she lived her remaining years in political obscurity. But she was not idle. She poured out her emotions and spiritual experience in letters and poems. She did not let up on her chiding of her son and he responded with calculated acts of cruelty. Elizabeth found solace in her Lord:

> Joyful will I be
> And bless his holy name.
> He is my help and stay
> And comfort in my shame.[5]

Towards the end Elizabeth, like her mother, suffered mental breakdown. Both ladies were uncompromising in matters of faith and morals. Having embraced evangelical Christianity, and being free from the political complications that necessarily governed the policies of their menfolk, they stuck to their beliefs with an unwavering, perhaps naïve, constancy.

The difficulty of wielding political authority without the power to determine policy is exemplified by Mary, Queen of Hungary and Regent of the Spanish Netherlands (1505–1558), Luther's most exalted female correspondent. Mary was the sister of no less a personage than Emperor Charles V. She was happily married to Ludwig II of Hungary and Bohemia but, in 1526, the king was killed in battle against the Turks. Luther, knowing that Mary had shown some sympathy towards the reformed cause, dedicated to her a commentary on *Four Psalms of Comfort*. But his attempt to draw her into the Protestant fold was doomed to failure. The defection of a Habsburg princess could not be tolerated by the family. Mary was dragooned into becoming Regent of the Spanish Netherlands, a responsibility she compared to having "a rope around my neck". The main cause of tension was the spread of Protestantism. Mary tended towards toleration and applied the law as leniently as possible, but her brother bullied her into submission, warning her that if she became a friend of Lutherans she would become his enemy.

Mary's position was impossible, as she frequently pointed out to her brother. Charles demanded draconian action against all who resisted Catholic faith. Mary lacked both the resources and the will to carry out her brother's instructions. She understood what Charles did not: that sincere people cannot be dragooned into abandoning their beliefs. Having asked several times to be relieved of her responsibilities, Mary was, at last, permitted to resign in 1555. The sufferings of men and women imprisoned or martyred for their faith have often been recorded. We should sometimes spare a thought for those who have found themselves stretched upon a cross whose two planks are politics and religion.

* * * * *

If we move further west we encounter more examples of the issues the Reformation created for female rulers and the ways they dealt with them. For the greater part of the sixteenth century France and its neighbouring principalities found themselves in a state of often violent turmoil, exacerbated, if not always directly caused, by the challenges emanating from the religious movements in Germany and Switzerland.

It was the death of Louis XII in 1515 that created a situation which brought to prominence a number of women destined to play important roles in the political and religious life of France. Louis left no male heir. The crown, therefore, passed to his distant cousin, the twenty-year-old Francis of Angoulème, who became Francis I of France. As well as continuing a long-running war with Spain, it was the new king's lot to cope with Europe's new religious divisions. Francis was a cultured and intelligent ruler who chose his councillors wisely – even if they were women! He was guided in the early years of his reign by his mother, the politically astute Louise of Savoy, who acted as regent when the king was away on campaign. But it was the king's elder sister, Margaret (1492–1549), who provided the creative energy of the royal household. She was both devout and intellectual and followed closely the controversial theological issues of the day. In these early years of the Reformation the scholarly world was abuzz with exciting new ideas, and few people were far-sighted enough to prophesy the fragmenting of Europe into rival politico-religious camps.

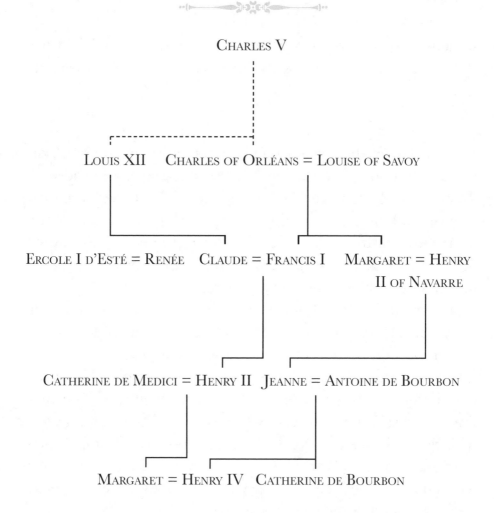

Hitherto, the international church had provided the framework for scholars who corresponded with each other and travelled from monastery to monastery to read the rare manuscripts housed in their libraries. The printing revolution changed everything. Intellectuals could read one another's works. This stimulated correspondence and the development of learned communities. No longer were these confined to members of the clergy. Royal and noble households enhanced their prestige by attracting celebrated scholars and thus becoming part of the international brotherhood of the learned. Heads of state no longer regarded themselves as outside the academic world. Henry VIII, who wrote a rebuttal of Luther's sacramental theology, was not the only ruler to enter the debating chamber. The courts of kings and aristocrats vied with each other to appear "cultured". What was remarkable was that women now gained admittance to this intellectual network.

Margaret's salon was soon renowned throughout Europe and was illuminated by several of the more avant-garde writers and thinkers of the day. The most famous was François Rabelais, the monk-cum-scholar-cum-doctor-cum-writer, popularly thought of as an apostle of hedonism. In fact, he brought gifts of wit and imagination to a traditional Catholic world in confusion. He satirized the establishment – particularly the religious establishment – and ruthlessly exposed hypocrisy. Margaret herself took a leaf from his book with her collection of bawdy tales called *The Heptameron* (published posthumously), in which she poked fun at errant clergy. Such works were very much in vogue. Sebastian Brandt's *Ship of Fools* and Desiderius Erasmus's *Praise of Folly* were just the lead sellers of a popular genre. Everyone enjoyed jokes at the expense of the ecclesiastical establishment. But Margaret and most members of her circle were in deadly earnest about the gap between Christian piety and what passed for orthodox religion. If they mocked bishops, schoolmen, and monks, it was in order to make people recognize just how critical the spiritual malaise was.

They did not set out to be heretics but it was inevitable that they would be interested in the challenge presented by Luther. Margaret translated into French the reformer's *Meditation on the Lord's Prayer* and certainly read his explosive *Babylonian Captivity of the Church*. She did not become a disciple of Luther but what she and members of her humanist coterie did was ask questions and refuse to accept, without comment, the Catholic party line. By the mid-1520s such free thinking was denounced as heresy. The early flickering of French Protestantism would certainly have been smothered were it not for the protection afforded by those like Margaret who were immune to attack.

She took as her spiritual director Guillaume Briçonnet, Bishop of Meaux, who headed the leading humanist cell in France, the Meaux Circle. Two of its more prominent members were Jacques Lefèvre d'Étaples, who produced the first French translation of the Bible, and the poet Clément Marot. Both men ran into difficulties with the ecclesiastical establishment for encouraging the study of Scripture in the original languages. When Marot lampooned the Paris schoolmen as ignoramuses, he was imprisoned and only the king's intervention saved him from a worse fate. Lefèvre was obliged to flee to Strasbourg. Throughout the 1520s the forces of reaction became entrenched. Critics were denounced as heretics. The upholders of tradition looked to the troubled state of Germany and warned the king what would happen if Lutherans and humanists were not forcefully suppressed. That the reform gained any ground at all in France is largely owing to Margaret's protection of evangelical activists in the early days of protest. Much to the frustration of church leaders, their complaints seldom outweighed the deep affection Francis had for his sister.

Though Margaret's personal religion was of a personal kind which would not be labelled "Lutheran" or "Calvinist", she certainly embraced the central Protestant doctrine of justification by only faith. Her own poetry reflected this:

To you I testify
That God does justify
Through Christ the man who sins.
But if he does not believe
And by faith receive
He shall have no peace,
From worry no surcease.

God will then relieve,
If faith will but believe
Through Christ the gentle Lord.[6]

Margaret's best known prose work was a little devotional manual entitled *The Mirror of the Sinful Soul*. It stands in the mystical tradition but its indebtedness to Luther is obvious, as for example in this extract, which treats of assurance and atonement:

The multitude of my sins are so hidden and overcome by thy great victory that thou wilt never remember them, for thou seest in me but the grace, gifts and virtues which it pleaseth thy goodness to give me. O, charity! I see well thy goodness doth consume my lewdness and maketh me a beautiful and godly creature. This that was man thou hast destroyed and made me so perfect a creature that thou hast done me as much good as any husband can do unto his wife, giving me a faithful hope in thy promises.[7]

No suggestion here of any dependence for salvation on the prayers of living priests or dead saints. This, too, was published posthumously, but became something of a classic among reformed Christians. In England, Princess Elizabeth made a translation for presentation to her stepmother, Queen Catherine Parr.

Whatever Margaret's private faith, she was a public figure. As her brother's closest adviser, but one whose sympathies lay with the radicals who were causing the government increasing problems, her position was a difficult one. She could not do what she helped some of her protégés to do – go into hiding or exile. Francis depended on her practical wisdom and her undoubted gifts as a diplomat, particularly when, having been captured by his enemies at the Battle of Pavia (1525), he relied on her to conduct the tricky negotiations for his release. Margaret was privileged by her position to be able to hold personal beliefs that were not wholly orthodox. Others were not as fortunate. As tension increased, evangelicals suffered increasing persecution. In 1525 the Meaux Circle was disbanded and Briçonnet himself faced heresy charges. This was the year of Margaret's marriage. Her husband was Henry II, ruler of the small Pyrenean kingdom of Navarre. Though she continued to visit her brother's court, her principal residence became Nérac in Navarre, from where she was less able to shield her protégés from attack.

It was another nine years before the storm broke in full fury, and when it did so it was not the reactionary clergy who were initially responsible. Some of the more zealous reformers decided on a public confrontation with the Catholic hierarchy (whom they unhesitatingly identified as the minions of the Antichrist). Dozens of them toured the streets of Paris by night putting up anti-Catholic posters. This "Affair of the Placards", coupled with the smashing of "superstitious" statues, was an outrage which could not be tolerated. Rebellion, for whatever motive, was an affront to the king, and Francis reacted firmly. Ringleaders were rounded up and burned in the Place Maubert.

Some protégés were difficult to help. Guillaume Farel was one of the members of the Meaux Circle whose enthusiasm was not tempered by discretion. Marked out for his fiery preaching, he was obliged to leave France and take refuge in Geneva. There, too, he fell foul of the authorities and was obliged to move on – but not before he had persuaded another talented French humanist to join him. Jean Calvin was a brilliant young scholar who had already published the first edition of his *Institution of the Christian Religion*, a systematic statement of reformed theology. It was the attempts of the two Frenchmen to enforce unanimity of belief and practice that led to their expulsion. In the overheated religious atmosphere of the 1530s, however, opinions changed rapidly, and by 1541 Calvin was back in Geneva, where he assumed leadership of the reformed church and its relationship with the state. Having worked out in detail the schema of reformed doctrine, Calvin was not disposed to be tolerant of any compromise. He urged leaders of other states to accept his teaching in detail. One on his correspondence list was Margaret. He castigated her for giving refuge to those of all shades of opinion and for not fostering "true" doctrine in France. She resented his hard-line approach, which showed no sympathy for her delicate position, but he continued to press her for greater commitment. The queen rose above resentment, reading Calvin's writings and even encouraging the use of his catechism, but not formally espousing his theology.

In the relative peace of Nérac Margaret found other ways of serving the reform. She welcomed Protestant fugitives, who found in the worship of her chapel biblical teaching and a congenial style of devotion. She became a kind of spiritual mother to the churches throughout her domain, visiting, encouraging, and providing written manuals on worship and doctrine. She kept up an extensive correspondence with members of a wide humanist and reformed network. Vittoria Colonna (see chapter five) was one of those with whom Margaret exchanged letters, and we can discern a distinctive kind of feminine spirituality in their epistles of mutual encouragement. In both reformed and unreformed churches it was taken as axiomatic that priests or preachers were those chosen by God to teach his flock, but Vittoria wrote about spiritual guides: "I believe that examples chosen from our own sex are always more fitting and following them is always more appropriate."[8]

Margaret died in 1549, before religion cleft France asunder into Catholic and Calvinist camps. It was still possible for such a prominent woman to preserve confessional neutrality. Yet, if she did not declare herself openly Protestant, it was not out of cowardice or political circumspection. Rather, it was because she found party labels irrelevant. Her faith was personal, even mystical, and was based on the Bible and the interior testimony of the Holy Spirit. This emerges clearly from her correspondence, such as this passage in a letter to Vittoria Colonna:

> *... your Adam with all his desires died and was crucified in our Lord Jesus Christ ... by whom you have been renewed in the Spirit – walking on a new earth, contemplating the new heaven, considering that the old external order of things has passed away ... and nothing will last except that which is interior ... no mortal thing is worthy of desire by those who have set their heart on the Eternal God ...* [9]

Jeanne d'Albret (1528–1572), the only child of Margaret and Henry of Navarre to survive infancy, grew up to share her mother's religious beliefs but not her eirenic demeanour. She had fierce convictions and stood by them stubbornly. Her determination and self-will were first put to the test in 1540, when she was married, on the orders of King Francis, to the Duke of Cleves. The eleven-year-old Jeanne protested loudly, shrilly, and persistently. She had to be carried, squirming, to the altar. Because of the bride's age the marriage was not immediately consummated and the couple lived apart. For five years Jeanne kept up her opposition and, surprisingly, she won. The union was annulled in 1545. Three years later Jeanne was married again to Antoine de Bourbon. Fortunately for everyone concerned, the bride was happy with her handsome young groom.

The independence of thought she had inherited from her mother led her to embrace Calvinism, and she was tutored in doctrine by Theodore Beza, Calvin's successor. She found the Genevan reformer's uncompromising, hard-edged theology to her liking and, once she was convinced of its truth, there was for her no question of modifying it. It was, however, 1560 before Jeanne made public confession of her faith. By this time both her parents were dead. Jeanne and Antoine were now the rulers of Navarre and their little state became the leading Protestant haven. Monasteries were closed, churches "purified", some Catholic rituals forbidden, and the New Testament was translated into the Basque language. A visitor from Geneva could report home, "Preaching is open ... The streets resound to the chanting of the Psalms. Religious books are sold freely and openly."[10]

The existence of a semi-independent heretic state within France could not be tolerated. Protestantism was now a major force in the land, with tens of thousands of converts. The challenge to the political and religious status quo could not be ignored. The government took up arms against the French Calvinists (Huguenots). Under pressure from the king, Antoine crumbled, and when the Wars of Religion began in 1562 he fought on the Catholic side. Jeanne was ordered to renounce her heresy and conform, but this lady was not for turning. She was still at heart the girl who had refused to submit to her first husband. Now she defied not only the new French king, Henry II, but also the pope and Philip II of Spain, the self-appointed champion of Catholic orthodoxy. Even though her four-year-old son was, for a while, held hostage in Paris and she herself was threatened with excommunication, abduction, trial by the Inquisition, and even assassination, Jeanne did not flinch. She improved the defences of her kingdom and confiscated Catholic church land, using the proceeds for poor relief and the setting up of a Calvinist academy.

France was now in the grip of a hatred as intense as can only occur when civil war is cloaked in religion. Fanatical generals urged their troops to face death in the name of God while the nation teetered on the edge of bankruptcy. Jeanne could not remain in the deep south, aloof from the military conflict. When the Protestant leader, the Prince of Condé, died (shamefully murdered by his captors while a prisoner of war), her son Henry became titular head of the Huguenot movement. Admiral Coligny, the military leader, established his base at La Rochelle on the Atlantic coast and the queen now moved to the Protestant HQ. From there Jeanne financed the movement and sent appeals for aid to foreign courts. She took no delight in Huguenot victories and appealed directly to the queen mother, Catherine de Medici, to grant freedom of Protestant worship and order an end to hostilities:

> *I implore you with tears and utter affection to make peace. Have pity on so much blood already shed which you can staunch with a word.*[11]

A fragile peace which secured a large measure of freedom for Calvinist worship was eventually signed at St Germain (1571).

Eager to follow it up with a move that would seal a more permanent settlement, Catherine proposed a marriage between her daughter, Margaret, and Henry of Navarre. Jeanne was torn between her desire for an end to hostilities and her mistrust of the royal court. She feared that once her son was in the queen mother's clutches he would be forced to renounce his faith. Nevertheless, she travelled through the snows of a bitter winter to the royal court at Blois to discuss the proposed marriage.

Jeanne was, by now, a sick woman. Her health had never been robust (which makes her iron tenacity the more remarkable), but now pain became a constant distraction as she faced the browbeating which Catherine and the Catholic leaders employed in order to gain the most favourable terms. Eventually, the other side resorted to blackmail. Jeanne's first, childhood, marriage had been annulled on the grounds of non-consummation. Now, Jeanne was told that the pope was ready to reverse the decision of his predecessor. That would have made Jeanne's second marriage adulterous and her son a bastard. Henry stood to lose all his inherited titles and property. The marriage agreement was signed in April 1572 and the ceremony fixed for 18 August.

Jeanne did not live to see it. She died on 9 June. In doing so she was spared having to witness the ultimate treachery of her Catholic adversaries. It may be that her demise actually encouraged Catherine de Medici to proceed with one of the blackest crimes in all European history. When French high society was gathered in Paris for the wedding which should have healed the nation's religious wounds, Coligny was murdered as the signal for an orgy of sectarian violence that spread over the whole country and became known as the St Bartholomew's Day Massacre (see chapter nine).

One person who received with particular grief the news of these terrible events was the elderly Renée de Valois (1510–1575), Duchess of Ferrara. She was the younger daughter of Louis XII and, as she once complained, "If I had a beard, I'd be the ruler of France." Had it not been for the Salic Law, the crown would have passed not to Francis I but, in turn, to Louis' daughter, Claude (died 1524), and then to Renée. France and Europe might, under these circumstances, have been saved a great deal of grief.

Renée was another member of the royal house who was won over to the new theology and suffered for it during the years that Catholic–Protestant tension built up. Young Renée, as a diminutive, plain, serious, and retiring teenager, had spent most of her time at Blois and other Loire chateaux. Many of her happiest hours had been spent in the company of Margaret de Valois and her stimulating intellectual friends. But princesses were not in command of their own destiny; they existed for the purpose of forging marriage alliances. In 1528, after a long and tortuous series of negotiations, eighteen-year-old Renée was engaged to the twenty-year-old Ercole d'Este, son and heir of Alfonse, Duke of Ferrara, and his wife, the notorious Lucrezia Borgia. She thus entered the sophisticated and politically complicated life of the Italian Renaissance city-states. Their married relationship was strained from the start. Renée was homesick, surrounded herself with French courtiers, and refused to learn the language of her adopted country. One of the ways her independent spirit revealed itself was in the bestowal of patronage. The encouraging and financing of artists and scholars was an essential part of the life of all rulers. Intelligent investment enabled talented craftsmen and intellectuals to make a living while, at the same time, enhancing the prestige of their backers. At no other time in the history of Europe was the relationship of patron and protégé more vital than during the Italian Renaissance. Over the years Renée brought to her court a cavalcade of men and women as talented as they were controversial. After the Affair of the Placards, Clément Marot was a marked man in Paris. Margaret of Angoulême advised him to seek refuge with Renée and he remained in Ferrara as the duchess's secretary until the situation in France cooled down, enabling him to return in 1539.

Like Margaret, Renée was not partisan in the extension of her protection – at least not openly so. Her official neutrality at a time when the leaders of Reform needed friends in high places irritated Calvin. He visited Ferrara in 1536 under the assumed name of Charles d'Esperville and spent long hours (followed up by a prolonged correspondence) trying to persuade Renée to nail her colours to the mast. She displayed her open-mindedness by welcoming to her court another – very different – celebrity of the age, Ignatius of Loyola, one of the great heroes of the Counter-Reformation. As a young man he had abandoned a military career and dedicated himself to the service of the church. Having been in France at the time of the Affair of the

Placards and become aware of the spread of evangelicalism, he conceived a heartfelt desire to protect the papacy from all heretical attacks. He gathered a small band of companions who would later become the Society of Jesus (Jesuits) and was attended by them on his visit to Ferrara. It was probably not obvious to observers at this tense and confused time that Renée's two guests were heading in opposite religious directions. They appeared as men of intense spirituality and zeal, concerned to cleanse the church's Augean Stables. No less than Calvin, Loyola wanted the backing of the duchess.

Such pressure was as nothing compared with the tactics her husband used to force her to conform to Catholic orthodoxy. Relations between Renée and Ercole deteriorated steadily. Had it not been for her close connection with the King of France, Ercole would have had no hesitation in denouncing his wife to the Inquisition. On one occasion he banished her to one of his castles for eighteen months. Matters took a decided turn for the worse after 1547, when Francis I died. He was followed to the grave by his sister two years later. The new regime in France was pro-Catholic, and Renée could no longer rely on the protection of powerful contacts. Ercole pressed home his advantage, using every tactic he could think of to force Renée to do the "respectable" thing of declaring loyalty to the pope. He negotiated the marriage of their eldest daughter, Anne, to Francis of Guise, whose family were the leaders of the French Catholics. He banished all his wife's Protestant friends and vigorously encouraged the Inquisition's purge of heretics throughout his territory. Still Renée refused to admit that she had anything of which to recant. If anything, the pressure clarified her thinking, so that she moved steadily towards the Calvinist position. Only when Ercole formally denounced her to the Inquisition, took away her remaining children, and made her a prisoner in her own home did she yield and abjure her

Protestantism. Even then, her recantation was nothing more than an outward display. She refused to attend Mass.

Her ordeal came to an end in 1559. That was the year Ercole died. His son took over as Alfonse II and he allowed his mother to return to her beloved France. She took up residence on her estate at Montargis, south of Fontainebleau. At last she was monarch of all she surveyed. Her home once again became a refuge for those fleeing from persecution – whether Protestant or Catholic. Despite her ecumenism (she even allowed her children to follow the denominational path of their own choosing), she asked Calvin to provide a pastor for her little flock. The man he sent was François de Morel, a scholarly Huguenot of noble birth. His presence at Montargis was a mixed blessing. He believed that it was his task to set up a church organization on the strict Genevan model. This would have involved Renée taking a very back seat, something she was not prepared to do. De Morel explained his predicament in irritated letters to Calvin. It was unthinkable, he protested, to permit women into the councils of the church. To do so would mean the reformed churches becoming "the laughing stock of Anabaptists and papists alike".[12] Renée was incredibly patient with de Morel and other ministers sent from Geneva but her frustration can be clearly observed in her continuing correspondence with Calvin. While always being courteous and grateful for his help, she pointed out, "It seems to me that so many ministers and people coming here, each one shouting his opinion, are unnecessary."

On 1 March 1562, Renée's son-in-law, now Duke of Guise, instigated the massacre of fifty Huguenots at Wassy, some 200 kilometres from Paris. His pregnant wife, Renée's daughter, was in her carriage nearby. The incident was "one of the great transformative events of European history, ushering in the age of the Wars of Religion, which … would engulf the whole of Europe".[13] Hatred breeds hatred. Francis, Duke of Guise, outlived the atrocity by less than a year before he was gunned down by an assassin. We can scarcely imagine the effect the news of these outrages involving her family must have had on Renée. They underscored in most cruel fashion her divided loyalties between kindred and faith. Under unremitting pressure from all sides she maintained a remarkable Christian charity. She refused to indulge in feelings of revenge and encouraged a forgiving spirit in others. She complained to Calvin about ministers who urged "simple women to kill and strangle": "This is not the rule of Christ. I say this out of the great affection which I hold for the Reformed religion." In discussing the Duke of Guise she rejected judgmentalism based on ill-informed prejudice: "He made it possible for me to harbour those of the Reformed religion in this village," she explained to Calvin. "I know that he persecuted, but I tell you freely that I do not know whether he is reproved by God for he gave sign to the contrary before dying".[14] It is impossible not to warm to this woman who, in the name of Christian charity and intellectual honesty, was prepared to stand up to the most celebrated Protestant thinker in Europe. Sadly, those in power did not share her eirenical spirit.

Renée lived long enough to witness France's implosion and the resulting religious and political chaos. In her own lands she maintained her authority and Montargis continued to be a refuge for men and women fleeing persecution. What is, perhaps, her most remarkable characteristic, bearing in mind the various pressures brought to bear upon her, is her spiritual integrity. This was something she shared with Margaret and Jeanne, and she was very conscious of a common bond with her royal relatives. In one of her letters to Calvin she wrote of Jeanne d'Albret:

As the late Queen of Navarre, her mother, was the first princess of the kingdom to favour the gospel, it may be that the present Queen of Navarre will complete the work by establishing it in her kingdom. She is well equal to that task. I love her with a mother's love and praise the graces God has bestowed upon her.[15]

These three French ladies provide us with a narrative which is easily overlooked and which enriches our understanding of the Reformation.

When Renée's daughter Anne married the Duke of Guise she became sister-in-law to another woman who had a significant role to play in the Reformation drama. But not in France. Mary of Guise (1515–1560) was the only daughter of Claude, Duke of Guise, head of France's most powerful noble family and one ardently dedicated to the protection of Catholicism. Her father earned the nickname of the "Great Butcher" because of his persecution of Lutherans in the 1520s.

Mary's troubles began in June 1537 when her husband, the Duke of Longueville, died. Theirs had been a happy but brief union and now, at the age of twenty-one, she was back on the marriage market. Within a year the contract was drawn up which united Mary with the recently widowed King James V of Scotland. It was a political deal, designed to curtail the ambitions and pretensions of the English king, but as the tumultuous century progressed, the alliance assumed a religious flavour.

Of the children born to James and Mary, only one daughter – Mary – survived. Six days after the birth, King James died. This raised the issue of who would effectively hold regency powers in Scotland. The nobility were divided into pro-English and pro-French camps. After years of intrigue, Cardinal David Beaton emerged as regent. However, the alliance of the queen mother and the cardinal was of short duration (1543–46). Mary worked with him and (with the aid of French advisers and, occasionally, French troops) managed the difficult task of controlling the rival factions, resisting diplomatic and military pressure from across the border, and aligning Scottish affairs with policy made in Paris. What complicated the political and diplomatic activities of Mary's government was the outbreak of a distinctive form of Protestant reformation. It rebelled against French Catholicism but did not embrace either Lutheranism or the brand of evangelical faith emerging in England. It was a particularly rigid form of Calvinism. The opening campaigns in the war between Mary's government and this new religious expression of Scottish nationalism were a preaching tour by the evangelist George Wishart in 1544–45, his arrest and public burning in 1546, and the retaliatory assassination of Cardinal Beaton. The following year Mary achieved full power as regent. At the age of five (in 1548), the infant queen was shipped off to France and pledged in marriage to the dauphin.

Mary's approach was conciliatory – both because she was not by nature obdurate and also because compromise offered the only possibility of preserving a unified Scotland for her daughter to rule. No fewer than three church councils were convened between 1552 and 1559 to discuss needed reforms. Unfortunately, events at home and abroad conspired against her. Mary Tudor's career as a persecutor in England (1553–1558) rang alarm bells north of the border. It also drove many Protestants to seek asylum with Protestant regimes abroad and to absorb the rigid theology and ecclesiology of Geneva and other evangelical communities. One of those who returned from exile was John Knox, who now travelled throughout much of Scotland demanding total rejection of anything that smacked of papistry. But even before Knox arrived the forces of change were being felt at grass-roots level, as he reported in a letter: "If I had not seen it with my own eyes … I could not have believed it … their fervency doth so ravish me."[16] The final misfortune was the sudden, unexpected death in July 1559 of Henry II in Paris. The dauphin now became king as Francis II, and his wife became queen. Since she was also Queen of Scots the two crowns were now linked, raising fears of Scotland becoming a French satellite.

But the long-threatened rebellion had already broken out. In March the Calvinist leaders, calling themselves the Lords of the Congregation, threatened Mary that if she persisted in making "ordinance against the Word of God, ye will provoke his wrath, and we of necessity must disobey your ordinance".[17] Simultaneously, mobs, egged on by Knox and other preachers, went on an iconoclastic rampage. Poor Mary had no option but to meet force with force. She brought more troops in from France. The Lords of the Congregation summoned military aid from England. Both sides shrank from full-scale civil war but military posturing prevented the conclusion of an agreed settlement.

Eventually, following the English pattern, it was the Scottish parliament which established a new religious identity for Scotland. With surprisingly little hassle, the members abolished papal jurisdiction and accepted a Calvinist confession of faith and a Presbyterian order of church government on the Genevan pattern. Mary of Guise was spared having to witness this crushing defeat of all she held dear. She died in June 1560, at the age of forty-four, worn out by her efforts to preserve the Old Alliance and the old faith.

CHAPTER 5

THE EDUCATED WOMAN

...even if the study of literature offers women no rewards or honours, I believe women must nonetheless pursue and embrace such studies alone for the pleasure and enjoyment they contain.[1]

In the late fifteenth century the idea of learning for learning's sake was novel. Study/training was linked to vocation. Tradesmen and artisans achieved the "freedom" of their guilds after long years of apprenticeship. Men who aspired to the higher learning of the universities did so in preparation for the roles they aimed to play as priests, diplomats, theologians, administrators, courtiers, bishops, lawyers, and teachers. It was the dissemination of the printed word, making available ancient texts and facilitating scholarly discourse, that gave rise to the Renaissance concept of the *uomo universale*, the complete civilized man whose mind was open to all knowledge. But if man was capable of enlightenment, why not woman? Indeed, there were fewer obstacles in the intellectual path of wealthy and cultured women than in that of their brothers and husbands. They had no professional expectations. They could not become the framers of political or economic policy. To that extent they were free to pursue any area of study that took their fancy. They could learn for the sheer pleasure of learning.

And a small but growing minority did so. The ladies in royal and noble households were able to surround themselves with musicians, poets, and scholars, to engage in intellectual debate and even to venture themselves into expressing their thoughts and feelings in the written word. The roll call of culturally influential women is varied and includes such diverse women as Isabella d'Este, Marchioness of Mantua, noted, among many other things, for founding a girls' school, and Tullia d'Aragona, who toured Renaissance courts as both a courtesan and an intellectual genius.

The words at the head of this chapter were spoken in a speech delivered in the University of Padua by a twenty-two-year-old woman. Cassandra Fedele (c.1465–1558) was a Venetian woman of distinguished family. She showed evidence of intellectual gifts from an early age. By the time she was twelve she had mastered Greek as well as Latin. Her father encouraged her and provided tutors who taught her philosophy, classical literature, and dialectics. By her mid-teens she was widely known as a prodigy, a woman who not only wrote poetry and prose but engaged in public debate with some of the best scholars of the day. Her father enjoyed showing her off. She enhanced his prestige and possibly brought him financial rewards. Her published works were read by intellectuals across Europe and Cassandra corresponded with several leading humanists. Queen Isabella of Castile tried to entice this phenomenon to her court.

Cassandra was not unique. A close contemporary was Laura Cereta, born in Brescia in 1469. She, too, was encouraged and taught by her father. Her *credo* was clearly stated in one of her letters: "For women who believe that study, hard work and vigilance will bring them sure praise, the road to attaining knowledge is broad."[2] If legend is to be believed, Laura actually taught moral philosophy at Padua University. She certainly published volumes of her letters.

These Italian ladies were not religious reformers or even proto-reformers. They are included here to show that in the Renaissance world there was room for female intellectuals. Yet what their stories also reveal is that such phenomena were abnormal and viewed in some quarters with suspicion. Cassandra's celebrity came to an abrupt end. In 1499 she married, and for the remainder of her long life she devoted herself to caring for her husband and running his household. This she saw as her vocation. Marriage ruled out the possibility of an independent career. Laura was "fortunate" in that, though she was married at the age of fifteen, her husband died within two years. She was then free again to follow the sacred path of learning – theoretically. In fact, she encountered a stone wall of prejudice. She was criticized for presuming to publish her own writings. Her faintly flickering flame guttered out with her early death in 1499.

Wide cultural interests and specific religious concerns could not be kept apart indefinitely as the Reformation storm intensified. We can see this in the career of Vittoria Colonna (1490–1547). She was one of the major celebrities of Renaissance Italy and we can still perceive something of her magnetic personality from a beautiful pencil sketch made by Michelangelo, who was devoted to her. She came from one of the leading noble families of Italy that had produced one pope and numerous church dignitaries. It was Vittoria's close knowledge of ecclesiastical affairs and her own deep spirituality that made her agonizingly aware of the failings of the church and drove her into the reforming camp.

When the breath of God that moves above the tide
Fans the embers of my smouldering state,

And the winds of God begin to dissipate
The foetid stench of the church, his bride,
Then the swaggering knights prepare to ride.
The war begins.[3]

Vittoria was as sickeningly aware as humanists and Protestants beyond the Alps that the times were out of joint and that the state of the church was a major part of the problem. She could get away with trenchant criticism in verse, prose, and letters because she was well connected, because her poetry was elegant and widely admired, and because she lived a life of exemplary piety. She received the conventional upbringing of a cultured lady of her class. She was privately tutored, read the classics, and met and corresponded with leading scholars and artists. At the age of nineteen (in 1509) she married Fernando d'Avalos, son of the Marquis of Pescara, to whom she had been betrothed in infancy. Her husband was a military leader, often absent on campaign. Vittoria saw him infrequently; they had no children, and Fernando died of wounds received in battle in 1525. Thereafter, Vittoria fended off numerous suitors and devoted her life to writing and private devotion. She became part of a multi-hued international network that included Margaret of Navarre (see chapter four), Cardinal Reginald Pole, the outlawed opponent of Henry VIII's religious policy, Michelangelo, Juan de Valdes, a free-thinking Spaniard who had fled to Naples to escape the Inquisition, and Bernardino Ochino.

Ochino (1487–1564) was a mendicant friar cast in the medieval ascetic mould. Finding the regime of his Franciscan order too lax, he had transferred to the new, austere Capuchin order and had risen, within a few years, to the position of vicar-general. He won fame throughout Italy as a preacher of intense spirituality. But, whatever his effects on his hearers, he was not at peace in himself. His experience, as he later described it, was remarkably similar to Luther's. Over-scrupulous self-examination and penance did not ease his soul:

I had departed further from God the more I tried to attain Him by storming Him by works. I was in dire confusion but I did not remain fixed at this point, for Christ revealed Himself to me in His grace, and when, with Paul, I forsook the trust in my own powers, I gained new confidence in God. I set all my hopes upon Him, and in all things gave myself up to His guidance, since I had only gone astray under my own. [4]

We tend to regard Luther's conversion experience as, if not unique, certainly uncommon, but there must have been many in these troubled years who felt the same despair at their own lack of spiritual progress and disillusion with the church's aids for the gaining of salvation. Like Luther, Ochino's quest eventually brought him to the haven of justification by grace through faith alone.

In a society in which gifted preachers were the celebrities of the age, Ochino attracted a considerable following. Men and women from all levels of society flocked to hear him and there developed a network of spiritually minded people eager for reform. Vittoria was a member of this avant-garde group of what we might call "evangelical Catholics". When, inevitably, Ochino and his brothers attracted the attention of the Inquisition, she sprang to their defence in a letter to Cardinal Gasparo Contarini, a member of the hierarchy committed to rapprochement between Rome and Wittenberg:

The Capuchins are accused of being Lutherans. If St. Francis was a heretic, then call them Lutherans. If to preach the liberty of the Spirit is a vice, when subject to the rule of the church, what will you make of the text, "The Spirit gives life?" If those who

*trouble these friars had seen their humility, poverty, obedience, and
charity they would be ashamed. As for obedience, they wish to
restore the rule of St. Francis. They are not rebellious against the
clergy. The charge is made that they do not obey their own general,
but he does not reform. The pope should support them. They want
freedom simply to follow the rule of their founder, and I do not see
why St. Francis should not receive as much favor at Rome as St.
Benedict. Francis did not enforce his rule by prisons and death, but
by humility, poverty, and love. I do not see why human arguments
should supersede the divine, that new laws should break the sacred
constitution of the church. We should not follow our own judgment,
but that of Christ and Paul.[5]*

Ochino fled across the Alps in 1542 but that was only the
beginning of his wanderings (both geographical and spiritual).
Over the next quarter of a century he travelled via Geneva,
Augsburg, London, and Zurich, finally fetching up among
anti-Trinitarian radicals in Poland. Despite his entreaties,
Vittoria declined to tread the same spiritual path. She never
left the Catholic fold but her beliefs went beyond the bounds of
orthodoxy, and it may well have been only her social standing
that protected her from investigation. Her poems leave us in no
doubt that she wrestled with central issues of the Reformation,
such as the relationship between faith and works:

*One cannot have a lively faith I trow
Of God's eternal promises if fear
Has left the warm heart chilled and seer
And placed a veil between the I and Thou.
Nor faith, which light and joy endow
And works, which in the course of love appear.
If oft some vile, deep dolor drear
Injects itself into the here and now.*

These human virtues, works and these desires
All operate the same, are but a shade.
Cast as a shadow, moving or at rest,
But when the light descends from heaven's fires
Kindling hope and faith within the breast
Then doubt and fear and dolor, these all fade.[6]

Vittoria Colonna was one of the few women who could indulge in the luxury of independent thought, but their numbers were growing. The baseline reason for this was that society was becoming more fluid. It is an obvious fact that women were subordinated to men. Marriage was the appointed lot of most women and, within that bond, obedience of wives to husbands was enjoined – by civil law, by canon law, by the doctors of the church, and by Scripture as traditionally interpreted. However, this was not institutional misogyny: the female half of European humankind was not singled out for suppression. *Everyone* had his/her preordained place in the social hierarchy. From pope and emperor down to the meanest peasant, all were cogs in a machine that would work properly only if each remained in its allotted position. This was the way God had designed things, and anyone who challenged his arrangements was guilty of heresy. People belonged to interlocking communities – families, clans, villages, manors, trade guilds, corporations, nations – and owed allegiance to their masters, landlords, municipal authorities, and kings. Social mobility was taboo. For example, anyone leaving his town or village in search of employment risked arrest and a sound beating (at least) for violating the strict vagrancy laws. Therefore, the reformers had to tread carefully in their teaching relating to women's place in society. The Peasants' War in Germany (1524–25) was just one example of how novel ideas (some with the alleged backing of Scripture) could undermine the entire social order. Protestant preachers and writers had to be careful about the implications or perceived implications of what they had to say about Christian liberty.

But the times they were a-changing. A vital element in the DNA of the Renaissance was individualism. Fifteenth-to-sixteenth-century thinkers did not, of course, invent the desire for personal freedom to question objective truth as defined by temporal and spiritual authorities, but they asserted it so firmly that there was never any possibility that Europe could retreat back into unquestioned authoritarianism. Humanism had much to do with the necessity of every man to develop his full potential. In the succinct words of Jacob Burckhardt, "man became a spiritual individual". And so did woman. One of the leading scholars of the age, the Christian Jew Juan Luis Vives, wrote his *Instruction of a Christian Woman* in 1523. Six years later it was translated into English and dedicated to Catherine of Aragon. Thereafter, it was never out of print, running to eight editions during the century. The treatise certainly did not advocate complete emancipation or sexual equality, but it did offer a new vision of the behaviour and education considered desirable for ladies of exalted status. It prescribed suitable classical and devotional texts – the writings of the more virtuous ancient authors and the doctors of the church. In Italy, as we have seen, gifted women were already appearing in public to give Latin orations and corresponding freely with leading intellectuals. Matters did not go that far in northern Europe, but in households where education was prized for its own sake and where women had the leisure for study, they were not averse to trampling down the barriers of prejudice.

Probably the most famous English "bluestocking" was Margaret More (1505–1544), daughter of the literary giant and royal councillor Sir Thomas More. Pious and well-read, Margaret became the first Englishwoman to have a work of translation published under her own name. *A Devout Treatise upon the Pater Noster* was a rendering into English of a work by her father's friend and Europe's most celebrated scholar, Desiderius Erasmus. Margaret corresponded frequently with Erasmus and he wrote for her a humorous dialogue in which he poked fun at traditionalists who wanted to keep women in "their place". Antronius (Ass) disputes with a learned lady, Magdalia, who proves more than a match for him:

A: Distaff and spindle are the proper equipment for women.

M: Isn't it a wife's business to manage the household and rear the children?

A: It is.

M: Do you think she can manage so big a job without wisdom?

A: I suppose not.

M: But books teach me wisdom.

A: … I could put up with books, but not Latin ones.

M: Why not?

A: Because that language isn't for women …

M: Is it fitting for a German woman to learn French?

A: Of course.

M: Why?

A: To talk with those who know French.

M: And you think it unsuitable for me to know Latin in order to converse daily with authors so numerous, so eloquent, so learned, so wise …?

A: Books ruin women's wits – which are none too plentiful anyway.[7]

It was exactly at the time when Margaret More was enjoying Erasmus's witty *The Abbot and the Learned Lady* (1524–25) that Luther was weighing up the pros and cons of marriage. He might well have been influenced by his friends Caspar and Elisabeth Cruciger. Caspar had been a student at Wittenberg, before becoming rector and preacher in St John's School at Magdeburg, some eighty kilometres down the Elbe. Elisabeth (1500–1535) was placed in a convent as a child but left when she was twenty-two. It was about the same time that she met Caspar. The two were married in 1524 and, four years later, moved permanently to Wittenberg when Caspar became a professor at the university. They and the Luthers were close friends until Elisabeth's death in 1535. The couples were united in marriage when the Crucigers' daughter became the wife of the eldest Luther boy, Johannes.

One thing that Elisabeth had in common with Luther was a love of music. They shared the conviction that hymns provided one of the best forms of religious education. Doctrinal truths, as well as the very words of Scripture, could be "sung into people's hearts". The treasury of vivid religious imagery set to music was established in the very early days of the Reformation. It was in 1524 that Luther published a book of eleven hymns – and one of them, "Lord Christ, the only Son of God", was by Elisabeth Cruciger. She was the first of many women who would contribute to the devotional life of the Reformation churches.

Music was part of the traditionally acceptable curriculum of women's education. It figured prominently in the lives of high-born ladies and also of religious communities. In noble households womenfolk were encouraged to become accomplished on the virginals or the lute and it was not only the popular love songs of the day that they learned. If they were educated in convent schools, as many of them were, they sang settings of the liturgical offices in Latin and devotional songs in the vernacular. Those who showed promise were particularly popular in the convents and might well be pressed into becoming permanent members of a community.

It was only natural that such women, when converted to Protestantism, should devote their talents to promoting their new faith. In Strasbourg, Catherine Zell (see above) published four small hymnals designed to introduce the tenets of the gospel to people at a modest price. Elizabeth, Duchess of Brandenburg, was another devotee of Luther, who corresponded with him and worked tirelessly to introduce the Reformation in the territories under her control (see below). Hers was a sad story and her devotion to the gospel cost her dear, but she turned her sufferings to good account in hymns and sacred verse:

Joyful will I be
And bless his holy name.
He is my help and stay
And comfort in my shame.[8]

One role women fell into very naturally was that of teacher. It was quite usual for parents to entrust the initial stages of their infants' education to nuns. We know, for example, that Thomas Cromwell, who in the 1530s was responsible for closing down all England's religious houses, was, a few years earlier, close friends with Margaret Vernon, Prioress of the Convent of Little Marlow, and that he entrusted the initial training of his young son, Gregory, to her and her sisters. Gregory was, at a very early age, sent to board at the convent.[9] In Lutheran lands acceptance of the new theology did not automatically lead to the closure of convents. Their potential value as educational centres and disseminators of reform was clearly recognized. In the 1540s Anna von Stolberg, abbess of the Saxon convent of Quedlinburg, obliged her colleagues to swear allegiance to Luther's Augsburg

Confession and the house became a very important school for both boys and girls.

In lay society also, women's roles in education developed in various ways. Educated women could now study the Scriptures just as much as their husbands, and many were encouraged to do so. Within their own households they often adopted the role of teacher. Since they were responsible for the spiritual and moral welfare of their servants it was natural for them to instruct their underlings in the ways of the Lord. Of course, they had to oversee the instruction of their children and tutor them in their catechisms. It was but a short step for Bible-reading housewives to include the children of friends and neighbours. Such activity, common throughout Europe, made it easy for many female gospel enthusiasts to morph from wives and mothers into educational activists who shared Bible truths with friends and neighbours, as well as their children. For some zealous women, missionary activity became more important than their domestic duties. Anne Askew, the "Fair Gospeller" (see below), left her stubbornly Catholic spouse and made her way to Lincoln Cathedral, where she stationed herself beside the newly installed English Bible and proceeded to expound it to any who would listen.

Such behaviour was, of course, abnormal and may in fact have been more of a hindrance than a help in gaining widespread acceptance of women as educators. Some, however, felt a real vocation for teaching. One such was Magdalena Heymair (c.1535–1586). We first discover her in the 1560s in the Bavarian city of Strasburg, where she was employed by Catherine von Degenberg, wife of the city's chief judge, as a tutor to her daughters. It was probably here that she met the man who became her husband, William Heymair, who was also a teacher. In the baroness's pious household the ladies read the Bible together. Reflecting later on their open-minded approach to the word of God, Magdalena wrote, "Eternal praise be to God, for I diligently considered Lady Degenberg's thought-provoking questions, and the Spirit of God often came to aid my contemplation, and led me into the truth."[10]

Neighbours joined them in Catherine von Degenberg's private quarters, or *Frauenzimmer,* a word which originally meant "ladies' room" but which in Lutheran circles came to have the connotation of a female fellowship group.

These gatherings of women for Bible study, prayer, and mutual encouragement have left virtually no records which would enable us to gauge how they operated or how widespread they were, but we can confidently state that they were extremely influential in establishing and deepening faith in homes throughout Protestant lands.* Johannes Mathesius, another of Luther's students, became pastor at Joachimstal, some seventy kilometres north of Berlin, and encouraged the establishment of *Frauenzimmer* groups in his parish. "Honourable matrons", he wrote, did not only learn God's word for their own benefit, "but also that they may teach their servants and children, be able to comfort their neighbours (both men and women) in sickness, childbirth, and otherwise."[11] In later years, when persecution became really serious, it was noted that women resisted reconversion to Catholicism more consistently than their husbands.

When the Catholic counter-attack hit Strasburg, Magdalena and her husband moved northwards to Cham, a town where evangelical influence had remained strong since the Hussite Wars of the previous century. Magdalena took up teaching in the girls' school. However, a change of regime obliged her

---

* This is particularly true of regions where the new doctrines were under attack by heresy hunters. Persecution always drives victims closer to one another for support and instruction. This was certainly true of pre-Reformation heretics such as the Lollards and the Hussites.

family to move on again. This time it was not Catholicism that she was fleeing but Calvinism. Frederick III, Elector Palatine, inherited a contentious quarrel between rival Protestant camps when he assumed power in 1559. After carefully weighing the arguments, this pious ruler gave his support to the Calvinists and ordained that their version of the gospel should be taught throughout his dominions. Magdalena and her husband relocated to Regensburg (1570), where, once again, she found a teaching post in a Lutheran school. By the end of her life, in 1586, she had moved again, to Košice in modern Slovakia, and was still teaching.

We would love to know more about this remarkable lady who, wherever she went, was determined to use her God-given gifts for the edification of the young. She had a sound grasp of Lutheran theology and did not hesitate to defend her pedagogic principles and methods by reference to the priesthood of all believers. Her fame, it seems, went before her, for she was always able to find employment. The city preacher of Cham, Willibald Ramsbeck, was fulsome in his praise:

> *In the number of holy Christian matrons, or God's prophetesses, who to be sure were also sinful and frail human beings … but cleansed by the blood of Christ and sanctified by the Holy Spirit, I not unjustly reckon the honourable, virtuous, and spirit-filled Frau Magdalena Heymair.*[12]

Magdalena explained her methods – particularly her use of popular song music as the setting for biblical lyrics – in books which went through numerous reprints and had the distinction of being placed on the Catholic index of prohibited books. Several of the children who were taught by her and by others who used her manuals went on to become leaders in church and state. It is quite impossible to gauge the influence of this remarkable woman on the religious life of Germany.

* * * * *

The two innovations that revolutionized life for many European women were new educational opportunities and access to the Bible. We might consider these as inestimable blessings, but for many they involved bewildering role changes, for some they involved suffering, and for a few they involved death. What they, as well as their brothers in the faith, had to struggle with was how to interpret the Bible and apply it to the contemporary social order. Scripture was not unambiguous. Luther's take on the creation narrative of Genesis (which was followed by most leading reformers) was that Adam and Eve were spiritually equal in that they both bore the divine image, enjoyed communion with God, and had been jointly charged with the oversight of the lesser creation. However, Eve had been made *for* Adam, as a companion and as a necessary partner in the business of populating the earth. Moreover, she had shown herself to be more vulnerable to temptation than her husband and, therefore, needed to be ruled and guided by him.[13] In the New Testament writings there was an obvious tension between the acceptance of first-century social conventions and the exercise of gifts bestowed by the Holy Spirit, irrespective of gender. Bible students did not need to look far beneath the surface of the epistles and the book of Acts to realize that women played various roles in the life of the early church.

Luther struggled to identify the implications of a faith which was, at root, *personal* but had to be lived out in a society whose structures were *institutional*. He was not afraid to tear holes in the social fabric by his rejection of the papacy, his opposition to monasticism, and his appeal to the nobility to endorse religious change, but he certainly did not want to throw the whole fabric away. He was careful to distinguish between changes arising naturally from the understanding of the gospel and changes originating in the ambitions of men (some of whom claimed to find sanction for their anarchic programmes in the gospel). The same difficulty was presented by women who believed that their newfound freedom in Christ would have an impact on their traditional roles. The result was inconsistency. The Bible had ordained that women should not preach to or rule over men – unless they received a special commission.

> *Each one should pay attention to his own commission and call,*
> *allowing another to discharge his office unmolested and in peace.*
> *As for the rest, he may be wise, teach, sing, read, interpret to*
> *his heart's content, in matters of his concern. If God wants to*
> *accomplish something over and beyond this order of offices and*
> *calling and raise up someone who is above the prophets, He will*
> *demonstrate with signs and deeds, just as He made the ass to speak*
> *and chastise his lord, the prophet Balaam [Num. 22:21ff]. When*
> *God does not do so we are to remain obedient to the office and*
> *authority already ordained.*[14]

What Luther did not say was how the church was supposed to recognize God's call to women to engage in novel ministries.

It was among the radical assemblies of the Reformation that egalitarianism was most stressed. By no means was there unanimity on this issue, but there was a broad agreement that the indwelling of the Holy Spirit freed believers from mere human institutions and conventions. In its extreme forms Anabaptism (and it must again be emphasized that this is an unsatisfactory blanket term) morphed into political anarchy and social unrest. Always Luther had at the back of his mind the horrors of the Peasants' War and attempts by preachers of violent apocalypse to set up "new Jerusalems". The most notorious was the commune established by Jan van Leiden in Münster (1534–35). This psychopath awarded himself sixteen wives, of whom the most senior, Divara von Haarlem, wore a crown and, as "Queen of Münster", shared his rule. Luther reserved his most trenchant criticisms for the deluded leaders of such movements who, he raged, deserved "death of body and soul". Such emotions came into play when he was confronted by those who wanted to make fundamental changes to the roles of women in society.

The majority of Anabaptist women were not Divaras. They were devout souls committed to Scripture and the inner testimony of the Holy Spirit. Hated by both Catholics and mainstream Protestants, they died in their hundreds, sometimes earning through martyrdom the respect and sympathy of those who rejected their theology. Such was the case of Maria and Ursula van Beckum, sisters-in-law who came from a wealthy Netherlands family. Their relatives were appalled that ladies from their own circle should adopt the beliefs usually associated with lower-class extremists. They were denounced by their own mothers, who were, doubtless, terrified of the backlash that would be felt by the whole family if the young women failed to recant. When Maria and Ursula were interrogated, the ecclesiastical authorities were impressed, not only by their steadfastness but also by their biblical knowledge and dialectical skill. Even a leading theologian brought in from Brussels could not shake their convictions. It was always an embarrassment when people of high birth and good education fell into heresy, and every effort was made to bring the women back to Catholic "truth". All was in vain. Maria and Ursula were burned at the stake in November 1544.

What makes their story particularly interesting is that these women found favour with Ludwig Rabus. Rabus was, for many years, a minister in Strasbourg and a rigid Lutheran. He fell out with Catherine Zell over her tolerant attitude towards

Anabaptists and was the leader of those critics who demanded that she should stop interfering in matters which, as a woman, were none of her concern. The bitter feud (bitter, at least, on Rabus's side) went on for years. Rabus was unsparing in his condemnation of those who erred from the Lutheran path. That makes it surprising that he recognized Maria and Ursula van Beckum as genuine Christians who suffered for their faith. Rabus devoted several years to producing a history of godly martyrs, beginning with Abel and continuing down to his own day. It was completed in 1557, a conventional work, similar to others written in these years by Protestant and Catholic authors eager to demonstrate the legitimate spiritual ancestry of their own church. And yet this out-and-out Lutheran found space for the sad story of the Anabaptist van Beckum ladies. The trials and tribulations of these devout upper-class women were so moving and so well known that he could not withhold from them their martyrs' crowns.

CHAPTER 6

WOMEN VENTURING INTO PRINT

If God has given grace to some good women, revealing to them by his holy scriptures something holy and good, should they hesitate to write, speak and declare it to one another because of the defamers of truth ... it would be foolish to hide the talent that God has given us.[1]

The Reformation was little more than twenty years old when Marie Dentière (see below), a French follower of Calvin, made this bold assertion of women's right to engage in written theological debate. Yet, although she clearly enunciated the principle, she was very far from being the first female writer to take up the pen in the Protestant cause. This phenomenon first appeared in the 1520s.

We have seen how literacy was working its way down the social strata; how some cultured women were joining the ranks of the literati; how wives and mothers were instructing their children and servants; how nuns released from the convent were taking up teaching roles; how churchgoers made notes of sermons and discussed them with members of their households; and how the goodwives of a village or urban district would meet to share their faith stories. Most of this activity took place in a domestic or neighbourhood setting and involved teaching and mutual encouragement between women. Wives and widows knew their place and did not venture into theological controversy with Catholic scholars. What happened in the 1520s, therefore, was nothing short of iconoclastic. It was not statues that were pulled down or windows smashed; the attack was on the ideological framework of society. Until Luther's challenge an enormous volume of discontent had been building up for several decades. The dam of clerical privilege and ecclesiastical power had successfully held back the pressure, but the attack from Wittenberg caused the first crack and what gushed forth from the widening fissure was a cascade of anti-establishment sentiment in various forms – theological tomes demanding doctrinal reform, anticlerical broadsides, satirical engravings, plays and poems by such masters as Holbein, Cranach, and Hans Sachs, and, eventually, peasant revolt. It is as part of this flood that the hitherto unimaginable phenomenon of female print campaigns must be seen.

What made it possible was the availability of vernacular Bibles and the ubiquity of the printing press. There was no town of any size in Europe which did not have at least one publishing house. Pamphlets were cheap to produce and, therefore, to sell. Just as today people (regardless of their expertise), rush to air their opinions via social media, so, 500 years ago, Christians with no theological training were eager to express themselves in print. Then, as now, sensationalism was big bucks and there was nothing more sensational than women writing trenchant polemic. The fundamental rationale of the Reformation made the appearance of these tracts not only possible, but inevitable. William Tyndale had vowed that he would make the plough boy better versed in Scripture than the average semi-educated priest. There was nothing to prevent literate housewives from also going to the fount of Christian truth or, if they were bold enough, from sharing their insights with any who cared to read. The early 1520s produced a flurry of Protestant pamphlets. Many – perhaps most – have not survived, but among those still available to us there are some interesting examples produced by women.

Argula von Stauff (c.1492–c.1563) was a lady of noble Bavarian stock who became a Lutheran devotee but whose faith was awakened before the reformer's works began to circulate. Her Christian understanding was deepened and widened by the new theology from Wittenberg but as a child she had been given a German Bible and studied it for herself. As a teenager she lost both her parents in an outbreak of plague and was placed in the household of Duchess Kunigunde of Austria, sister of the emperor Maximilian. This cultured lady was accomplished and well-read and a patroness of scholars, including humanists. She recognized Argula's keen intellect and encouraged her spirit of enquiry. In 1516 a husband was found for her and she moved to Dietfurt, near Ingolstadt, as the wife of Friedrich von Grumbach. As soon as Luther's arguments with papal authorities began, Argula took a deep interest, writing to the leaders at Wittenberg and elsewhere. She was eager for all news about the spreading controversy. One of her informants was her younger brother, Marcellus, who was a law student at Ingolstadt.

It was Marcellus who brought Argula the news, in 1523, that was to launch her on her brief literary career. He reported how a fellow student, Arsacius Seehofer, had fallen foul of the university authorities. When Lutheran works were found at his lodging, the young man was forced to recant his "heresies" and sent to a Benedictine monastery to, as we might say, "have his head sorted out". This was a critical period for the city and the university. Luther's books were circulating and had already made an impact, but the reformers reckoned without Johann Eck, the leading member of the theology faculty and Luther's most implacable enemy. It was he who instigated the persecution to which Seehofer fell victim.

Argula was so incensed by the injustice and cruelty of the young man's treatment that she wrote a long letter to the university and demanded a public debate on the issues raised. She circulated handwritten copies of her protest. Friends in the great imperial city of Nuremberg had the letter printed as a pamphlet. It became an instant sensation. It went through fourteen reprints in two months. Such effrontery and such success were extraordinary. A woman – a self-taught woman with no convent training and no credentials as a devotional author – had dared to challenge the leading Catholic scholars of Germany!

What this indicated – perhaps more vividly even than the spread of Luther's writings – was that an exposed nerve had been struck. Argula had written what many people were thinking but dared not say. She was like the little boy in the story of the emperor's new clothes: she pointed out the obvious. The main points she made were as follows: 1. The Bible is the sole arbiter of Christian truth and conduct. 2. Luther and his associates were pre-eminently expounders of the Bible. 3. Compelling belief by means of threats, imprisonment, and execution was alien to the gospel. The tone of Argula's tract was vigorous and uncompromising:

> In the German writings of Luther and Melanchthon I have found nothing heretical ... Even if Luther should recant, what he has said would still be the word of God ... You have the key of knowledge and you close the kingdom of heaven ... I write as a member of the Church of Christ against which the gates of hell shall not prevail, as they will against the Church of Rome.[2]

Argula was fully aware that she was flouting convention but she made no apology for doing so.

> *I am not unacquainted with the word of Paul that women should be silent in church (1 Tim. 1:2) but, when no man will or can speak, I am driven by the word of the Lord when he said, "He who confesses me on earth, him will I confess and he who denies me, him will I deny" (Matt. 10, Luke 9).*[3]

Not content with this direct challenge to the university, Argula used her social and political contacts to seek support from William IV, Duke of Bavaria. She exploited the tensions between church and state authorities by giving voice to fierce anticlericalism. She called upon William to use his position to further the work of reform. She urged the closure of monasteries and the employment of their confiscated resources in the relief of the poor. She demanded an improvement in the educational standard of parish clergy and, above all, that they should be sacked if they failed to preach the gospel. Her hopes were probably based on her earlier knowledge of the duke. He had originally welcomed the Lutheran movement but the swelling tide of criticism, complaint, and protest convinced him that the demand for religious change was an attack on the whole establishment. He went onto the defensive and, after the outbreak of the Peasants' War in 1524, he became a major player in the Counter-Reformation.

Argula was nothing if not thorough. She approached any individuals or powerful political group who might help. To the city fathers of Ingolstadt she expounded the doctrine of the priesthood of all believers. To Frederick the Wise, Elector of Saxony and Luther's patron, she pleaded the cause of the poor who were deprived of Bible-based preaching. What she wrote she was prepared to declare openly in public. She rode to Nuremberg, where the Imperial Diet was in session, though, frustratingly, we do not know what she did there or how she was received.

She made it clear in some of her published letters that she expected and was prepared to embrace martyrdom. Quite why she was not arrested and tried for heresy is not known. The only action taken by her enemies was to order her husband to control her. This he was, apparently, quite unable to do. He was even sacked from his job for not disciplining his unruly wife. Argula heard rumours that Friedrich had been ordered to cut off her fingers to stop her writing or even to wall her up alive. She was denounced from pulpits in violent language. "Arrogant devil", "heretical bitch", and "shameless whore" were just some of the insults thrown against her. She was certainly an embarrassment to her family. She wrote to a relative to defend her actions – though "defend" is scarcely an appropriate word to describe her stance:

> ... *my dear cousin, take it not amiss if you hear that I confess Christ. I count it a great honour to be reviled for his sake ... I hear you have heard that my husband has locked me up. Not that but he does much to persecute Christ in me. At this point I cannot obey him. We are bound to forsake father, mother, brother, sister, child, body and life ... I understand that my husband will be deposed from his office. I can't help it. God will feed my children as he feeds the birds and will clothe them as the lilies of the field. My dearly beloved cousin, I commend you to God's grace that you may dwell with him now and forever.* [4]

Despite what this letter might suggest, Argula did not desert her husband and their four children. Unlike some Protestant women, she did not claim scriptural support for leaving an unbelieving spouse. Friedrich died in 1532. After a brief second marriage Argula remained a widow. Her literary activities ended as suddenly as they had begun but she remained an outspoken and troublesome woman until the end of her days. Her enemies never knew quite what to do with this forthright harridan whose behaviour bordered on the eccentric. Ridicule did not work because she was always ready with jibes of her own. To respond to her arguments would give the impression that they took them seriously. The safest option was to ignore her, and it was probably for this reason that she disappeared from the limelight. Possibly, also, the later history of Arsacius Seehofer, whose misfortunes had lured Argula into print, had a bearing. He escaped from his confinement and became an itinerant preacher. He no longer needed an advocate.

Another woman who entered the fray at the same time was Ursula (c.1500–c.1566), the wife of Johann Weyda, a middle-ranking Saxon government official. What aroused the ire of this feisty lady was a diatribe against Luther published in 1524 by Simon Plick, Abbot of Pegau, a monastery near Leipzig. His language was far from moderate and Ursula repaid him in his own coin. The ensuing exchange had much in common with a street-market slanging match. Ursula denounced the abbot as a half-witted drunk who knew less about the Bible than a cow knew about dancing. The more reasoned parts of her argument were against monasticism and chastity – an unnatural state, the imposition of which, she insisted, could and did create problems.

In the white heat of the pamphlet war Ursula was soon answered. Whether she ventured into print again is not clear but supporters certainly waded in with fresh contributions. *An Apologia for the Wife of the Tax Collector of Eisenberg* was published anonymously in 1524. It added nothing to the theological debate but it did strongly take up the cause of women writers. Scripture, it claimed, endorsed their endeavours. Had not the Virgin Mary composed the *Magnificat*? Did not the prophet Joel declare that daughters as well as sons would proclaim divine judgment in the last days? Philip's daughters had been prophetesses. Certainly, Paul had stated that women should not be allowed to speak to and for the church. But because there were now insufficient men ready to proclaim God's message he was raising up women to help carry the burden.

We have already encountered Catherine Zell and her sharing of her husband's ministry in Strasbourg (see chapter two), but she did not restrict her activity to the local church. She, too, entered the pamphlet war of the 1520s. Her first essay was a defence of her marriage to a priest – *Catherine Schütz's Apologia for Master Matthias Zell, her Husband*. She was "stung" into this public reaction by the insults, lies, and sniggering innuendos of those who opposed the marriage of monks, nuns, and priests. "It is proper to (and part of) being a Christian to suffer," she wrote, "but it is not at all proper to be silent, for that silence is half a confession that the lies are true."[5] Catherine's defence of married clergy led her on to define Christian discipleship as embracing all who believed in Christ, thus endorsing Luther's insistence that baptism, not ordination, was the sacramental entry to ministry. This necessarily implied that she had the right to interpret Scripture and to correct interpretations she considered erroneous. That led on to criticism of several contemporary practices. As she had married a priest, it was understandable that she should attack clerical celibacy. She hit out at homosexual practices and at the system of cohabitation fines by which, for a fee, bishops pardoned priests for the sin of concubinage.

If we may judge by the works that have survived, 1525 seems to mark a hiatus in the literary output of Protestant women. The two most likely reasons for this are the Peasants' War and the spread of radicalism. Both were an embarrassment to Luther and his colleagues. Catholic propagandists were quick to blame the breakdown of civil order on the new heresy. Luther responded by writing one of his most violent denunciations – *Against the Murderous and Thieving Hordes of Peasants* – and he urged the German nobility to suppress the insurgency without mercy.

As regards the radicals, Luther was determined to distance himself from them and to show that his teaching did not unpick the threads binding church and state. He denounced them as fanatics. Several strands of extreme teaching developed at an early stage and displayed that fragmentation to which evangelicalism is prone. Some rejected infant baptism; some were pacifists; some rejected the swearing of oaths; some set more store by ecstatic utterances than by the Bible; some were preachers of fiery apocalyptic prophecies. All were, in varying degrees, antisocial; some, indeed, claimed that only by separating themselves from the world and actively inviting persecution could Christians prove they were sincere in their faith. Luther denounced them all as fanatics and had no hesitation in asserting that they were just as much children of Satan as were his "papist" adversaries.

Catherine Zell, as we have seen, was to the fore in welcoming and assisting radicals who sought refuge in Strasbourg. Because of its comparatively tolerant attitude, the city attracted large numbers of people on the Protestant fringe. There were as many as 2,000 "Anabaptists" there by 1530 and among their congregations a large number of "prophetesses" were to be found. We have already encountered some of these charismatic ladies (see chapter three) but it is appropriate to include one of their number here too, because her visions and messages were recorded in print.

Ursula Jost was born around the turn of the century and, by the 1520s, was married to a butcher, Lienhard Jost, and living in a village not far from Strasbourg. Lienhard had the gift of prophecy and seems to have attracted the attention of the authorities, for he suffered a spell in prison. Perhaps this is why the couple moved to a house within the city walls, where they were living by 1524. Ursula specifically and earnestly sought to share her husband's mystical experiences.

> *After my husband and spouse was released from custody and was let go, he and I together prayed earnestly and diligently to God, the almighty merciful Father, that he would let me also see the wondrous deeds of his hand. God's grace and kindness granted this to us, and these visions written down here all appeared to me. I saw all these visions and wonders in the glory of the Lord, which always unfolded itself before me. And in it I received knowledge of the meaning of these visions of divine wonders.*[6]

Ursula's visions rapidly gained her a following and, around 1530, she published an account of seventy-seven of them, entitled *Prophetic Visions and Revelations of the Workings of God in These Last Days, revealed through the Holy Spirit from 1524 to 1530 to a Lover of God.* A first impression of these "revelations" is that they were not "prophetic" in the sense of specific messages given to the faithful relating to current or imminent events. They were very much generalized "pictures" of divine glory and judgment in the pattern of the biblical book of Revelation – and just as mysterious. A couple of examples convey the tone of the whole pamphlet:

> *… the glory of the Lord again approached me and unfolded. In it I saw a pretty green tree, which had many thousands of green branches. And I saw that out of the tree sprang a fountain. Then I saw two men coming who were well-dressed. They picked up a pretty green piece of sod from the ground. And I saw that with it they struck the fountain and stopped it up. Then I saw that the water of this fountain rose and flowed out to the branches a thousandfold. And then I saw that there came a great host of*

people who were from the common folk. They drank the drops
that ran off the branches, and they were all satisfied. And I saw
that they had raised their hands and their heads to God the eternal
Father, and to him gave the highest praise and thanks.
 ... I saw in the sky many guns, large and small. Between them
I saw a path adorned with brightness and with many colours.
And it was extremely narrow. And I also saw clouds which were
entirely the colour of blood.[7]

Members of Ursula's community would have been able to
relate these revelations to their own circumstances. They were a
persecuted people who drew comfort from such assurances that
they belonged to God's world, the greater reality, and that in the
imminent judgment they would be numbered among the elect,
while all the adherents of false religion and no religion would
suffer appalling punishments.

Like the more "central" evangelicals, the radicals rejected
the magisterial authority of the Catholic hierarchy. Unlike
other Protestants, they looked for their authority not (or not
solely) to the written word of God, but to direct communication
with the Almighty via charismatic celebrities. Since God was
no respecter of persons and reckoned all believers to be equal,
there was scope for women to take their place as teachers,
guides, and inspirers of God's people. Prophetesses, like their
male counterparts, were self-authenticating. The forcefulness
of their personalities and their manifest sincerity ensured
them a following. The fact that their impact was personal
and direct probably explains why few of them committed
their prophecies to writing. They were not, as it were,
"confined" to a literary medium. Their effectiveness lay not in
interpreting Scripture and applying it to current conflicts, but
in demonstrating the presence of God with his chosen people
through signs and wonders.

To Luther and those who looked to him for their theological understanding, anything that could not be justified by the clear word of Scripture had to be rejected. To him the Bible was quite clear about the position of women. In Eden woman had been created as a "helpmeet" for man and her descendants were to share this subordinate position. The apostle Paul had indicated how this relationship should play out in the church. For fifteen centuries the church had mirrored the ordering of secular society in this regard, and the reformers saw no reason to challenge this tradition. Luther

> *... did not grant equality to women in religious matters. When some of the radicals permitted women to preach, Luther found the idea ridiculous. A woman's place is in the home, he said. Women ... have no understanding, and when they attempt to speak about serious things they speak foolishness.*[8]

As we have seen, Reformation leaders actively encouraged women in positions of political authority to support Protestant individuals and churches. In the first flush of ecclesiological upheaval they were ready to accept the contribution of female pamphleteers. But the threatened dislocation of society in 1524–25 drove them onto the defensive and made them distance themselves from women who sought to "usurp" the teaching role reserved for men.

The female writer who most flagrantly challenged traditional gender stereotypes was Marie Dentière (c.1495–c.1561). She is the nearest thing to a feminist campaigner produced by the Reformation. When Luther's writings began to circulate she was a nun living in an Augustinian house at Tournai, and was one of the many to abandon her original vocation as a result of what she read. She married an ex-priest, Simon Robert, and the two of them moved to Strasbourg, that tolerant haven of early religious dissidents. Husband and wife worked together in spreading the reformed faith until Simon's death in 1533, by which time Marie had five small children to look after. Within two years she had remarried another Protestant activist, Antoine Froment, and they set up home in Geneva about the time that Calvin began his ministry there (1536).

We know very little about Marie's life but it seems that she was a member of Margaret of Navarre's circle (see above). The queen was godmother to one of Marie's children and the relationship was sufficiently close for Margaret to ask Mme Froment for information about the troubled events in Geneva. The Reformation there had got off to a very rocky start. Calvin's plans for the government of the city and the relationship between the civic authorities and the pastors were too rigid for the moderate Protestant members of the council. After a bitter war of words the reformer had been expelled from the city. Margaret was anxious about dissensions within the reformist camp. She wanted details from Marie and Marie was more than ready to provide them – or, at least, her version of them.

The evangelical challenge had begun in 1532 with the arrival of Guillaume Farel and his associates preaching reform. This led to "shoutings and shootings" as Catholic and Protestant partisans clashed ever more violently. The reformers won and the local bishop was deposed by the civic authorities. He reappeared at the head of an army but was defeated by the new order with help from the city of Berne. These events had been described by Marie in an anonymous pamphlet, *The Fight for the Delivery of the City of Geneva, Faithfully Told and Written Down by a Merchant Living in that City*. It was not so much a historical work as a vindication of the reformers who, as the outcome demonstrated, were obviously on the side of the angels. The chronicle was, she averred,

> *... a very eloquent thing for all those who love God and His Word,*
> *and it is for them a great consolation to uncover, to open, to see, to*
> *tell, and to speak; but for all their enemies, traitors and adversaries*
> *of God and of this city, it is a great desolation, ignominy and*
> *confusion ... it is always God's work to show His virtue and power*
> *in things considered hopeless by men, so that that honour and glory*
> *is provided by Him for all, although it belongs to Him. For He has*
> *no regard for the number or force of His adversaries, but only for the*
> *faith and confidence that one has in Him ...* [9]

It was after their initial victory that the reformers began falling out among themselves and it was this that led to the banishment of Calvin and Farel in 1538.

Marie responded to Queen Margaret's request for information with a second pamphlet designed for wide publication. This time she had more windmills at which to tilt, as its title made clear: *A Most Beneficial Letter Prepared and Written Down by a Christian Woman of Tournai and Sent to the Queen of Navarre, Sister of the King of France, Against the Turks, the Jews, the Infidels, the False Christians, the Anabaptists and the Lutherans.* The author urged Margaret to use her influence with the king to put an end to dissension among Christians. But what she had in mind was not toleration. She believed that Calvin's understanding of the gospel, the organization of the church, and the establishment of a Christian commonwealth was divinely inspired and that any deviation from his system was heresy. She hoped to see Calvin restored to Geneva to continue the work which had been interrupted (he eventually came back in 1541).

But Marie had another axe to grind – freedom and equality for women in the church. She had disguised her identity in the first book by assuming the *nom de plume* of an anonymous Genevan merchant. She knew that the leaders of church and state would be scandalized by the temerity of a woman blundering into the male precincts of theology. By 1539, when she sent the *Beneficial Letter* to the press, she had thrown off any such deference to convention. Marie's way of life – leaving the convent, openly proclaiming her faith, publicly interpreting the Scriptures – had aroused controversy and involved her in arguments with both men and women in the reformed church. This had given her boldness to demand change in the attitude to women in the Christian commonwealth of Geneva. Now she opposed, in print, "any of the faithful who say that women are very impudent in interpreting Scripture for one another". She catalogued the outstanding women of both Old and New Testaments whose exploits were applauded. She demanded to know

> *[w]hat preacheress has done more than the Samaritan woman, who was not ashamed to preach Jesus and his word, confessing it openly before all the world as soon as she heard from Jesus that one must adore God in spirit and in truth. Or is anyone other than Mary Magdalene … able to boast of having had the first revelation of the great mystery of Jesus' resurrection …*

And she went on to point out that it was not a woman who had betrayed Jesus to the authorities.[10]

This really put the cat among the pigeons. Such behaviour could only play into the enemy's hands. Those who opposed the reform movement portrayed it as subversive, an irreligious challenge to the divine ordering of society. Calvin himself was among those who believed in the superiority of men. Despite the fact that Marie Dentière had championed his cause, the spiritual leader of the Genevan reform did not support her. In fact, from the scant evidence we have, it seems likely that he found her a nuisance. His relationship with the city authorities was still difficult. If Marie's tongue was as sharp as her pen, Calvin may well have regarded her as an embarrassment. In later years he ridiculed her unlicensed preaching, criticism of church officers, and presumptuous claim of equality with men. For whatever reasons, no one, apparently, came to her aid when council agents swooped on the printing house where her pamphlet was being produced. All copies of her work were confiscated and the printer was arrested. It was not only in Catholic lands that censorship operated. While reformed thinkers could find an audience for their revolutionary new theology, demanding any re-evaluation of the social structure was completely taboo.

Someone who was careful not to make this mistake (and who probably owed her life to being cautious) was Catherine Parr (1513–1548), the last wife of England's Henry VIII. Henry made her his queen in 1543 when he was already a semi-invalid in constant pain, and, as his close advisers and attendants well knew, could not be expected to live very much longer. He was almost certain to be succeeded by his only son, Edward, who at the time of Catherine's marriage was a five-year-old. This meant, inevitably, that the kingdom's religious and political destiny would be in the hands of whoever could dominate the regency of the underage king. Two court factions jostled for power – a reactionary group determined to prevent England from sliding into heresy and an evangelical group who regarded the work of the Reformation as unfinished. Because Catherine was known to incline to the latter, she became a target for the Catholic councillors, led by the Duke of Norfolk and Bishop Gardiner of Winchester, to attack.

Catherine was studiously non-political but her religious sympathies were clear, and politics and religion were inseparably intertwined. Her closest companions were ladies committed to further reform, such as the Dowager Duchess of Suffolk (see chapter two). Thomas Cranmer and Hugh Latimer (both destined to become Protestant martyrs) were among her spiritual advisers. Her own convictions (like those of most thinking people in this time of theological effervescence) were still developing. She had absorbed from the humanist critique of Erasmus a commitment to the primacy of Scripture and had probably already come to accept the Lutheran doctrine of salvation by faith only. Norfolk and Winchester regarded the new queen as a threat and resolved, in 1546, to disgrace her.

There were two ways to discredit Catherine in her husband's eyes. One was to convince him that she was a supporter of convicted heretics. The other was to show that, as a "mere woman", she had ideas above her station and was presuming to lecture others – including her husband – on matters of religion. The first part of the plot failed lamentably. The plotters brought to trial a zealous Lincolnshire gentlewoman by the name of Anne Askew. Once her examiners had established that Anne was, indeed, a heretic, they tried, by increasingly desperate means (including torture), to force her to name her "accomplices". Anne had court connections and had been helped by members of the queen's circle but she refused to turn informer.

The second line of attack was more promising. Catherine was in the habit of discussing matters of religion with her husband. Exactly what subjects she brought up we do not know. In her own quarters she presided over prayers and Bible studies, encouraging members of her household to embrace evangelical faith. She may well have conceived it to be her Christian duty to bring Henry also (or especially) to a "knowledge of the truth". One day she went a bit too far, causing a tetchy Henry to mutter sarcastically "it is … a thing much to my comfort, to come in mine old days to be taught of my wife".[11] Gardiner, hearing this, grabbed his opportunity to point out the disruptive effects of evangelical heresy. This, he pointed out, was precisely the sort of socially corrosive behaviour associated with evangelical "covens". Henry, always highly sensitive about anything touching his honour, sanctioned a covert investigation of Catherine's religious opinions. Fortunately, she got wind of the plot and, in an urgently arranged tête-à-tête with her husband, she disavowed anything as "unseemly and preposterous" as for a wife "to take upon her the office of an instructor or teacher to her lord and husband". If she had encouraged Henry to discuss religion with her, it was, she said, in order to distract him from his pain and also so that *she* could learn from *him*. All was forgiven, and it was the conspirators who felt the rough end of Henry's tongue.

Had Catherine's enemies been allowed to search her quarters for incriminating evidence, this crisis might have had a very different outcome. They might well have discovered not only books by reforming theologians, but notes in the queen's own hand, setting out her own faith. For Catherine Parr was an author. Indeed, she was the first English woman to publish under her own name. Her earlier works had been devotional manuals, such as translations of the Psalms and a book of prayers. But the book she was working on in 1546 was more personal and made clear her theological position.

The Lamentation or Complaint of a Sinner was published at the urging of the Dowager Duchess of Suffolk and others some months after Henry VIII's death (in January 1547) and promotes, without ambiguity, the evangelicalism favoured by the regime which was, by then, in power. It is a spiritual autobiography similar to Margaret of Navarre's *Mirror of a Sinful Soul* (a translation of which Catherine had received from Princess Elizabeth two years earlier). The author confesses the blindness of her earlier years when she tried to justify herself by "works religion". Then she discovered, as Luther had earlier discovered, imputed righteousness. She calls it "infused faith":

> *Then began I to perceive that Christ was my only Saviour and Redeemer, and the same doctrine to be all divine, holy, and*

*heavenly, infused by grace into the hearts of the faithful. Which
never can be attained by human doctrine, wit, nor reason, although
they should travail and labour for the same to the end of the world.
Then began I to dwell in God by charity, knowing by the loving
charity of God, in the remission of my sins, that God is charity, as
Saint John saith.*[12]

The *Lamentation* was more than a personal journal. The author
was eager to point out how easily her readers might go astray:

> *... many will wonder and marvel at this my saying, that I
> never knew Christ for my Saviour and Redeemer until this time.
> For many have this opinion, saying, Who knoweth not there is
> a Christ? Who, being a Christian, doth not confess Him his
> Saviour? And, thus [mistaking] their dead, human, historical
> faith and knowledge (which they have learned in their scholastical
> books) [for] the true, infused faith and knowledge of Christ,
> which may be had (as I said before) ... And true it is, except they
> have this faith, the which I have declared here before, they shall
> never be justified.*[13]

England was, by now, moving rapidly along the Reformation
path but Catherine was not destined to see it. She died of
puerperal fever in September 1548.

The story of the last of our female writers takes us back to the
court of Ercole II of Ferrara and his duchess, Renée (see chapter
four). In 1539, long before the ducal couple fell out over religion,
a bright local teenager was brought into the court to act as tutor/
companion to their young daughter, Anne. Olympia Morata
(1526–1555) grew up in an intellectual environment and her own
literary gifts became obvious at an early age. She took no delight
in "girly" pursuits, as she made clear in one of her poems:

I admire the flowery meadows of the Muses,
And the pleasant choruses of twin-peaked Parnassus.
Other women perhaps delight in other things.
These are my glory, these my delight.[14]

Her reputation as a child prodigy was soon recognized and she was paraded in the salons of fashionable ladies and gentlemen who were amused by the facility with which she could converse in Latin and Greek.

Thanks to Renée's encouragement, the classroom became a place for the discussion of the fashionable "New Learning", a term which embraced everything from classical studies to evangelical religion and which was distinct from the old intellectual and spiritual disciplines. Gradually, Olympia, like other humanists, was drawn into the evangelical fold. It seemed the logical destination, and the increasingly fierce opposition of Rome reinforced the conviction that the reactionaries were resorting to persecution because they could not win the argument for resisting reform. It was a stimulating atmosphere for a clever young woman to grow up in. But that atmosphere was to change.

For some months in her early twenties Olympia had to spend her time at home looking after her dying father. When in 1549 she tried to return to court, she was brusquely excluded. Duke Ercole, aided by agents of the Inquisition, had virtually completed his purge of religious dissidents. He was still unable to break his wife's spirit and force her to recant, but she could no longer protect her co-religionists. But this was not the only thing that distressed Olympia. Her friend and classmate, Anne d'Esté, had just been married and left Italy for France. The news about her which reached Olympia was not good. Her husband was Francis de Guise (he became Duke of Guise in 1550), the man who led the anti-Protestant campaign in France with unremitting vigour. But what hurt Olympia most deeply was that she was rebuffed by the duchess, who had been turned against her by a vicious whispering campaign. That, at least, was how the situation appeared to the young woman who now found herself devoid of influential friends. Doubtless, the truth was more complex. Religious opinion in Ferrara was now polarized. Olympia was known to have consorted with radical thinkers whose orthodoxy was, to say the least, suspect. Celio Secundo Curione, a scholar friend of Olympia's father, had had several brushes with the ecclesiastical authorities, was known to have been in contact with Anabaptist groups, and had been hounded out of Italy by the Inquisition. More recently, Fassio Fanini, one of the many young men influenced by the reformist monk Bernardino Ochino (see chapter seven), had been arrested on the orders of Duke Ercole for preaching against the doctrines of the Mass and prayers to the saints. Members of Olympia's circle interceded for the prisoner and she was in danger of being identified with a condemned heretic, since it was standard procedure for detainees to be examined and tortured in order to reveal the names of their supporters (Fanini was eventually burned in Ferrara in September 1550).

Olympia had also made friends with a group of German scholars who had come to Ferrara to continue their studies. She married one of them, a brilliant intellectual like herself, by the name of Andreas Grunthler. With him she gladly escaped to Schweinfurt, a Bavarian town which had declared for the Reformation. Never did she abandon her studies and, increasingly, her overwhelming concern was the spread of the gospel, particularly in her native land. She set herself to master German in order to translate the works of Luther into Italian. She used her academic contacts to urge other scholars to provide similar texts to help spread evangelical doctrine. She employed any literary device that might convey the truths she wished to pass on – including fiction. A dialogue between two women, Theophila ("Lover of God") and Philotina ("Lover of worldly praise") was intended to impress on readers the importance of coveting heavenly rather than worldly treasure:

> *T: Nothing is more splendid and magnificent than the heavenly kingdom.*
>
> *P: I know, but there were some saintly women who had the good things of this life as well …*
>
> *T: God gives to some and withholds from others, and it is not for us to judge. His greatest gift is himself …*
>
> *P: These troubles of mine seem little to you. You'd feel differently in my shoes.*
>
> *T: … To any of us may come sickness, ignominy, poverty, hate, dissension, torments of the spirit greater than those of the flesh. The Christian must be ready to bear his cross.*
>
> *P: I would rather suffer here than hereafter.*
>
> *T: Anything is more tolerable if it is brief and this life is short.*[15]

Olympia did not shrink from admonishing her social superiors. When she heard of the persecution unleashed by the Guise faction in France, she wrote to her erstwhile classmate, Anne d'Esté, now Duchess of Guise. She insisted forthrightly that it was her old friend's duty to plead with her husband for clemency towards the suffering Protestants:

Perhaps you will say, "If I do that, I may make the king or my husband angry with me and may make new enemies." Think that it is better to be hated by men than by God, Who is able to torture not just the body but also the soul in perpetual fire. But if you have Him as a friend, no-one will be able to harm you, unless He permits it, in whose hands all things are. See to it that you think on these things.[16]

There can have been few people and probably no women who wrote in that vein to one of the most powerful ladies in France.

Olympia and her husband were not destined to enjoy peace in Schweinfurt for long. The religious/territorial wars of German princes and nobles raged back and forth over the area. The town came under siege more than once, its people suffering terrible privations. Eventually it was burned down and the Grunthlers were among those obliged to flee with nothing but the clothes they stood up in. Friends and co-religionists helped them in their wanderings and eventually they reached Heidelberg, where Andreas was offered a post at the university. The hardships of the journey took their toll on Olympia's health. Yet through all her sufferings she kept up a large correspondence, begging books from other scholars, describing her own tribulations, giving spiritual counsel, and encouraging her friends to remain true to their faith. After her death, her husband sent to Curione, then a professor in Basel, all the writings of his wife that he could find, and Curione published them. Much had been lost in the couple's wanderings. What survived were dialogues in Latin and Greek, several poems, Psalm translations, and letters. It is these, the letters, which give us particular insights into the scattered community of Italian Protestant exiles as well as Olympia's character.

As soon as she arrived in Schweinfurt she wrote to Matthias Flacius. This scholar had been born in Istria and pursued his studies, bent on an ecclesiastical career. His academic path led him, via Basel and Tübingen, to Wittenberg, where he was appointed Professor of Hebrew. Inevitably, he fell under Luther's spell, but did not accept the reformer's teaching hook, line, and sinker. It was his determination to retain his intellectual independence that led him to move on from Wittenberg and, subsequently, from various other centres of learning where he tried to teach his own brand of Protestantism. However, much of this peregrination lay in the future when Olympia wrote to him in 1555.

> *My dear Sir ... you were the first to come into my mind as one who seemed able to help my fellow Italians, who are lost in so many errors and are in need of the good things of heaven. If you were to translate into Italian any of Luther's German books in which he argues against the general errors ... or if you would write something in Italian on the same subject ... I am sure that you would save many pious men from the errors by which they are misled.[17]*

She similarly entreated Pier Paolo Vergerio, a Venetian career ecclesiastic, who had tried to be a peacemaker between Rome and Wittenberg but had ventured too close to the latter, fled across the Alps, and been condemned as a heretic *in absentia*. From Vergerio Olympia received details of the theological divisions in the reformed camp, particularly over the Lord's Supper. She was not sympathetic to the disputants. "I think it could easily be resolved", she wrote, "if men would consider not their own glory but that of Christ and the salvation of the church, which includes concord."[18] Curione dedicated Olympia's collected works to another mutual friend, Isabella Bresegna (1510–1567). This wealthy Neapolitan lady was one of the many influenced by Ochino in the 1530s. Twenty years later, when she was the wife of the Governor of Piacenza, her house became a meeting place for evangelicals. Mounting opposition obliged her to escape to

Switzerland. When her husband begged her to return she replied that she could not live in a land where liberty of conscience was denied. Having abandoned the costly comforts and the status of a leading figure in Italian society, Isabella became reliant on the support of fellow exiles and eventually settled in Zurich when Ochino was a leader of the church there.

Through Olympia's letters we gain a vivid impression of a religious diaspora – men, women, and sometimes children hustled from their homes because of their convictions, eagerly exchanging news, offering encouragement, and urging steadfastness. Olympia's account of her own troubles is poignant, but what she experienced undoubtedly was not unique, and her sufferings cast light on an overlooked aspect of sixteenth-century religious history. Her physical pain only added to the mental anguish of permanent separation from her mother and other members of her family. Forced to flee barefoot from Schweinfurt wearing only a shirt, she knew deep despair: "I said to myself, 'This is all I can take. I am going to lie down here and die.' Then I said, 'Lord, if it is thy will that I live, give thine angels charge over me that they may lift me up upon their wings. I just can't make it.'" Writing to her sister, she reflected that her experiences were shared by many others:

> *There is trouble everywhere. Germany is raped. England suffers persecution. Ochino has fled to Geneva. Oh my dear sister, may I be able to pray with David in the 90th Psalm, "Teach us to number our days that we may get us a heart of wisdom". Remembering that the span of our life is but toil and trouble and we soon fly away, may I give myself to the contemplation of things eternal.[19]*

In a letter to Curione in the autumn of 1555 she reported that she was sick with a fever:

But there is still a spirit in my body that remembers all my friends and the kindness they have shown. So to you and those kind men who have blessed me with so many lovely gifts I wanted to give great thanks, if the fates had allowed. I think I am going to depart soon. I commend the church to you, that whatever you do be of use to her. Be well, my dear Callus, and don't grieve when my death is reported to you, for I know that then, at last, I shall live and desire to be dissolved and to be with Christ.[20]

This was her last letter. Olympia Morata died in October 1555. She was twenty-nine.

CHAPTER 7

PATRONS AND PROTÉGÉS

The glue that held together the highly stratified society of Renaissance Europe was patronage. Ambitious scholars, artists, and clerics seeking advancement thronged the courts of the rich and powerful, hoping for employment or for financial handouts to put food on the table while they completed their masterworks. What they offered in return were original works of artistic, literary or scholarly merit that would add lustre to the courts where they were employed and win praise for the cultured taste of their patrons. Thus, for example, Hans Holbein the Younger, after long years establishing his career in Basel, travelled to France and tried, unsuccessfully, to commend himself to King Francis I. Thereafter, with the help of an introduction from Erasmus, he obtained the backing of Sir Thomas More, one of Henry VIII's councillors. This led eventually to his employment by the English king and his appointment as official court painter. The support given to struggling artists, writers, jewellers, and craftsmen of all kinds was not mere charitable activity; patronage was a two-way system. When a king or an aristocrat agreed to be "good lord" to an aspiring artisan, that artisan pledged himself to serve his patron in whatever ways were demanded of him. In Holbein's case that included illustrating government propaganda pamphlets and even spying on potential enemies of the regime.

In the case of religious teachers and preachers, their activities might embrace anything from conducting family worship and providing personal spiritual counsel to teaching the children of the household or even running a local school. In return, the protégé enjoyed a measure of protection from ecclesiastical and civic authorities and freedom to preach. Throughout the Reformation years many evangelical leaders relied on well-placed society women for support. We have already seen how Luther and Calvin sought the help and protection of noble and royal ladies for themselves and for preachers sent to propagate their reform programmes, but the phenomenon was much more widespread. Indeed, for many women eager to spread the reformed faith but unable because of social constraints to take on the roles of preacher and teacher, supporting reformist clergy was the only way they could serve the gospel.

The story of Bernardino Ochino provides a good example of a reforming career aided at several points by admiring female patrons. He spent most of the early sixteenth century in Siena as a member of the Observant Franciscans, that element of the order dedicated to ensuring strict conformity with rules laid down by the founder. Partly in response to the spread of Protestantism there arose within the order a faction dedicated to engagement in theological controversy, backed by even more extreme ascetic practices. In 1528 the devotees of this holiness movement were authorized as a separate body, the Capuchins, and within a few years Ochino had joined it. From the beginning there was bad blood between traditional Franciscans and those demanding further reform. The Capuchins owed their very existence to powerful friends such as Caterina Cibo, Giulia Gonzaga, Vittoria Colonna, and Renée of Ferrara.

Caterina Cibo (1501–1557) was Duchess of Camerino, an independent commune in central Italy. She was related to the Medici on her mother's side and had three popes among her close relatives. This meant that from her earliest years she was caught up in the vigorous and often violent politics of the region. More than once she had to flee her home when Camerino was attacked by enemies. She was inevitably involved in intrigue, especially after the death of her husband in 1527. Caterina became increasingly disillusioned with morally decadent clergy who schemed and lied for material gain and paid scant heed to the plight of the poor. She was attracted to those religious who set examples of holy living and preached the need for reform. The traditionalists used every means including imprisonment and physical violence to silence the critics. At this point Caterina came to the aid of the reformers by appealing directly to her uncle, Pope Clement VII. As mentioned above, it was largely thanks to her intervention that the Capuchin order came into being.

But the tribulations of the zealots were not over. Their enemies kept up a relentless campaign to have the new order closed down. Caterina, despite having her own political problems to contend with, continued to support the Capuchins, but her influence diminished after the death of Clement VII in 1534. Months later, she was obliged to cede power in Camerino to Guidobaldo della Rovere, who had married her daughter Giulia, the heir to the duchy. She withdrew to Florence and it was there that she renewed and strengthened her friendship with Ochino. His thinking had moved steadily in a "Protestant" direction. He joined the Capuchins and, in 1538, became general of the order. He was now fifty-three years of age but his remarkable Reformation career was only just beginning. Ochino had always been an electrifying preacher. As he tramped the rutted highways and city streets of Italy, crowds flocked to hear this bare-footed friar with the austere countenance and long white beard. Caterina was only one of several prominent members of society who were captivated by him. Constantly reflecting on Scripture, his theological viewpoint changed continuously. From its source in Franciscan mysticism the river of his contemplation was fed by radical tributaries, and by 1538 elements of Lutheran *solafideism* could be discerned in his preaching. It was this gradualism that made him a potential threat to the defenders of Catholic orthodoxy. A charismatic preacher with a large influential following (including some cardinals) could be apprehended only if he were propagating manifest heresy. But the Inquisition did keep a wary eye on Bernardino Ochino.

Caterina supported him openly, providing food and lodging in Florence and financial help for his travels. She also consulted him freely. She allowed the friar to publish some of their conversations for the edification of other seekers after truth. A brief quotation gives us a taste of these dialogues. The lady begs to know how she can love God. Ochino advises her to become a nun. When she balks at this, he explains that a true devotee does not need to join an order. What is important is not donning a habit but assuming the apparel of inner holiness. Caterina responds eagerly:

> *I, Caterina Cibo, Duchess of Camerino, testify that I now take the three vows. The first is poverty. I will live without love of any created thing. The second is obedience to all the laws of the spirit. The third is chastity, that my mind may be immaculate and free from whatever is displeasing to God. I will regard him as my father, Christ as my brother and the Holy Spirit as my spouse. I will hold myself ready to endure martyrdoms, pangs, infamy, exiles, imprisonments, persecutions, crosses, and deaths insofar as I am able. I will cast myself wholly into the arms of the crucified, through whom alone I hope for the pardon of my transgressions.*[1]

Giulia Gonzaga (1512/13–1566) married at fourteen and was widowed at sixteen, inheriting her husband's fortune. As well as being wealthy, she was widely regarded as one of the great beauties of the day. Unsurprisingly, she spent much of her time fending off suitors. But she was no recluse. Her villa near Naples was open to scholars and preachers of all stamps and her salon was a centre of humanist free thinking. It was about 1534 that she heard Ochino preach and was profoundly moved to consider the state of her immortal soul. She took up residence in a convent in Naples but did not live there as a professed nun. From there she kept up a lively correspondence with reformist thinkers. She exchanged books (including Calvin's) with other members of the network and, from her largesse, she helped people who were fleeing from the authorities.

The Neapolitan circle drew into itself a variety of men and women seeking something conventional church life could not offer. As we have seen, they became known as *Spirituali*.

Divergent themes naturally emerged from such a creative and articulate group, yet central was a renewed emphasis on the grace which God sent through faith, together with a consistent urge to reveal the Holy Spirit as the force conveying this grace.[2]

A leading figure in the group was Juan de Valdes, a Spanish courtier and humanist scholar who had fled from his own country to escape the Inquisition. In Naples he, like Giulia, experienced a life-changing revelation as a result of Ochino's preaching. It was natural that Giulia should help him with her fortune and her influence. She belonged to one of Italy's leading families and her cousin was Cardinal Ercile Gonzaga, one of the more reformist members of the College of Cardinals. Patron and protégé exchanged letters and Valdes composed longer expositions for Giulia. It was for her that he wrote *The Christian*

Alphabet, a tract that provides an insight into the faith issues that both of them were wrestling with.

The treatise did not set out to attack Catholic doctrine and practice but, in that it stressed the inwardness of religion and took the Bible as its sole authority, it inevitably challenged the official teaching of the Church. Valdes urged his patron to meditate on the *schema* of salvation as described by St Paul. He advised her against reposing trust in outward rites and ceremonies. Giulia should not concern herself with her own eternal destiny, he counselled, but respond in thankful faith to what God in Christ had done for her. Assured of her redemption, she should continue to produce the fruit of good works. Nor, he was bold to say, should she allow the fact that she was a woman to deter her from exploring and sharing her faith. St Paul's strictures against women preaching, he said, applied only to wives, who were bound to be led in matters spiritual as well as temporal by their husbands. As a widow, such restrictions did not apply to Giulia.

All this was dangerous stuff, too close for comfort to the teaching emanating from Wittenberg, Geneva, and Strasbourg. The Neapolitan circle came under increasingly close scrutiny from the Roman Inquisition, especially after 1555, when arch-heresy-hunter Cardinal Caraffa became pope as Paul IV. Attempts were made to force Giulia out of the safety of the convent. They were unsuccessful.

Ochino, meanwhile, had continued his peripatetic teaching, his fame going before him in the letters circulating round Italy from his patrons. It was largely thanks to Vittoria Colonna (see above) that he was welcomed in Venice, where he spent a long sojourn from 1539 to 1542. From there Cardinal Bembo, a leading scholar of independent mind, reported to Vittoria in glowing terms: "Our Fra Bernardino is literally adored here. There is no-one who does not praise him to the skies. How deeply his words penetrate, how elevating and comforting his discourses!"[3]

It was not true that "everyone" praised him, though. Agents of the Inquisition were watching him closely and, in 1542, he was ordered to present himself in Rome for interrogation. He set out in obedience to the papal summons but, in Florence, he was warned to proceed no further. Caterina Cibo was among those who pressed him to flee Italy and provided him with clothes and money. One of Vittoria Colonna's relatives gave him a horse and a servant. Thus equipped, Ochino travelled to Ferrara. Here he was welcomed by Duchess Renée (see chapter four), who furnished him with more necessities and may have given him a letter of introduction to her friend Jean Calvin.

Now the Capuchin friar removed his cowl and threw himself wholeheartedly into the life of the reformed churches. In Geneva he took a wife and started a family. He turned to writing and issued numerous theological treatises. But he did not find among the northern Protestants the unqualified acceptance he might have hoped for. Having adopted a questioning attitude to the dogmas of the Catholic Church, he could not accept unequivocally the diktats of Calvin and other evangelical leaders. He moved from one centre of reform to another, fetching up in England in 1548, at the invitation of Archbishop Cranmer.

Ochino's travels were symptomatic of an extraordinary pattern of migration that characterized life in mid-sixteenth-century Europe. As the forces of reaction got their act together and instigated co-ordinated counter-attacks on the reform movement, and evangelical regimes hit back, substantial numbers of refugees moved to and fro across national borders. It is estimated that some 4,000 Protestant refugees arrived in England during the reign of Edward VI (1547–1553), creating the kind of social and political problems always connected with large-scale immigration. Cranmer and his colleagues on the council of the boy king were intent on setting up a godly commonwealth. They eagerly welcomed continental reformers who could help them complete the transformation of the English church. As in Italy, Ochino found himself idolized and supported by an evangelical network, many of whose members were women.

One young lady who associated closely with Ochino was the highly educated Anne Cooke, soon to become Anne Bacon (see chapter two). She was twenty-two when he arrived and had already read some of his printed works, being, as she was, well versed in Italian. Before Ochino had been in England six months a book containing translations of five of his sermons was in circulation. They dealt with justification by faith, the basic doctrine being propagated by the government as it sought to establish the Protestant Reformation. Though anonymous, this is generally believed to be the work of Anne Bacon.

There is no doubt about the authorship of fourteen more translated sermons published in 1551 and attributed to "A.C.". The principal doctrine set forth in this volume was predestination, indicative of Ochino's embracing of Calvinism. Anne was involved, with other scholars, in publicizing Ochino's work, and further editions of his sermons appeared until 1570. Clearly, Anne was as enamoured of his teaching as members of the Neapolitan circle had been.

Ochino's English sojourn was not destined to last. The remaining decade of his life was doomed to be sad and increasingly lonely. There were two reasons for this. One was the accession of Mary Tudor in 1553 (see chapter nine), a queen determined to eradicate all traces of evangelical religion. Now the migratory movement went into reverse. Most of the foreigners fled the Catholic regime and were joined by English Protestants, seeking havens in Geneva, Zurich, Strasbourg, and other cities where the reform was well established. Ochino's travels took him to Geneva, Chiavenna, Basel, Zurich, Nuremberg, Poland, and Moravia. The other reason for his restlessness was the onward rush of his theology. His reflections on Christian truth led him to embrace certain Anabaptist tenets and perhaps also antitrinitarianism. Every Protestant church was establishing its own orthodoxy and the free-thinking Ochino seldom stayed anywhere long without upsetting his hosts.

While in Zurich (1561–63) he met up with an old admirer and member of the Neapolitan circle. Isabella Bresegna who had fled there from Piacenza (see above).

Isabella had headed first for German Lutheran territory, before moving to Zurich. Though her circumstances were considerably reduced, she was by no means poverty-stricken, and was able to maintain a modest household thanks, in part, to a pension provided by Giulia Gonzaga. She joined the Italian church of which Ochino was the pastor. He thought very highly of her and dedicated to her a treatise on the Lord's Supper. She was, indeed, a kindred spirit who had embraced voluntary exile for her faith. Isabella also became the dedicatee of the collected works of Olympia Morata, edited by another banished Italian scholar. Indeed, as a lone woman, her courage and determination were of an even higher order. Ochino applauded this in his dedicatory epistle:

> *A spirit so exalted and a mind so clear as yours could not remain buried beneath the papist stupidity and when Christ had opened your eyes you perceived the abominable superstitions, idolatry and anti-Christian blasphemies of Rome. You decided to forsake all to embrace Christ.*[4]

Unfortunately, Isabella was no more able than Ochino to accept all aspects of Zwinglian doctrine and within months she had moved on to Chiavenna. Her distraught family begged her to return to Piacenza but her response was the same to every entreaty – she could not live in a land where freedom of conscience was not permitted. One of her sons did eventually join her and this was some consolation for her in what remained of her earthly life.

When she died, in 1567, Ochino had been dead for some three years. He found no peace at the end. His uncompromising and ever-shifting theology would not allow him to submit to the authority of any church leader. Driven from Zurich, he found temporary sanctuary in Nuremberg but was there accused of atheism and obliged to move on to Cracow. He narrowly survived a brush with the plague, which took away three of his four children. His eventful life came to an end at Schlackau in Moravia, where he was lodging in the house of an Anabaptist protector. Close to the end, he was questioned about which church he really belonged to. His reply was: "I don't want to be associated with any party; I want to be simply a Christian." In the boiling cauldron of the Reformation years, things were not that simple. Perhaps they never are. We can only hope that in his last, lonely days he found comfort in the memories of all the friends who had helped, supported, and inspired him. Many of them were women.

Ochino's story is a dramatic illustration of the vital, though unquantifiable, contribution women of "quality" played in the spread of reformist doctrine. Debarred, themselves, from public preaching, they could and did support the endeavours of teachers and evangelists of whom they approved. One of the noble ladies who succoured Ochino was Catherine, Duchess of Suffolk, who, as we have seen, later experienced a similarly peripatetic career because of her commitment to the gospel (see chapter two).

This feisty lady played a crucial role in the spread of the Reformation in England during the years preceding her exile. As a habitué of the royal court on friendly terms with Henry VIII (her husband Charles Brandon, Duke of Suffolk, had been the husband of the king's sister, Mary, who died in 1533), she was in a position to advance the careers of evangelical scholars and clergy. Hugh Latimer, the most famous English preacher of the early Reformation, often preached to Catherine's household. It was not always a comfortable experience. On at least one occasion the duchess, a wealthy fashionista, had to listen to Latimer's attacks on vain displays of sartorial extravagance. A more pointed sermon was directed at women who failed to "keep their tongues in better order". Catherine was famous (or notorious) for expressing her opinions and criticisms very forcibly.

But her influence and forthrightness by and large benefited the evangelical cause. As well as paying itinerant preachers and appointing evangelical incumbents to the many churches in her gift, she encouraged "lectureships" or "exercises". These were gatherings of clergy who, from about 1550, met to receive instruction in Calvinist theology. Catherine knew that the only way to secure the Reformation was to implant it in the hearts and minds of ordinary people through regular biblical exegesis. If England changed from a Catholic to a Protestant country, as it did over a period of several decades, it was due in no small measure to men and women who used their authority in the shires to ensure that evangelical doctrine was regularly taught wherever their writ ran.

There was a strong international element to Catherine's patronage. Ochino was not the only foreigner to enjoy her bounty. She helped prominent evangelicals and found benefices for men such as Martin Bucer and John à Lasco, who arrived either seeking asylum or at the invitation of English church leaders. In the reign of Edward VI she was instrumental in securing the site of the Austin Friars' London house as a worship centre for Dutch and French fugitives, even though their liturgy and doctrine did not square at all points with English practice.

When Mary Tudor came to the throne official policy did a 180-degree turn. Now it was Englishmen who were being arrested or fleeing abroad. In the months before her own departure Catherine was assiduous in sending money, clothes, and food to those who were imprisoned for their faith. Bishop Nicholas Ridley (subsequently burned at the stake) acknowledged a gift of "six ryals, six shillings and eight pence" for himself and fellow prisoners. This money (equivalent to, perhaps, £1,000 in modern terms) would have been used not only for necessities but also for bribing guards to allow visitors and obtaining writing materials so that the incarcerated could continue their ministry from their cells. Some bought new clothes to wear at their execution in order to show that, far from being dejected, they saw themselves as going to a heavenly party. Catherine also attended to the needs of families left behind when the head of their household went into exile.

She was not alone. In fact, one of the intriguing elements in this story of female patronage is that its participants formed a wide charity network – a kind of sixteenth-century Mothers' Union! Women of means played a vital role in the survival and strengthening of the early Protestant church in England, though information on their activities can only be glimpsed here and there in surviving records. They

> developed intimate relationships with each other as they built the church. They pooled their resources to support poorer brothers and sisters, formed groups to pray for imprisoned believers, and sheltered evangelicals persecuted by the government.[5]

One of the more remarkable features of this network in an age of rigid social division was that it embraced women of different classes. Several of the Duchess of Suffolk's "sisters" were of gentry or mercantile stock.

One indication of the importance of this female "underground" is the disquietude it provoked among some of their protégés. Ministers, theologians, and preachers were grateful for the assistance of women and many expressed their gratitude in fulsome letters. However, the very fact that they were beholden to women was an embarrassment. Some felt it necessary to remind their benefactors of their subordinate status. While accepting material relief with one hand, they wrote letters of disapprobation with the other. They pointed out that it was not part of women's role to enter into theological debate – a sure sign that some ladies were doing just that. Catherine Willoughby, Duchess of Suffolk, was certainly one such. On her return to England in Elizabeth's reign she engaged in heated correspondence with William Cecil, the Secretary of State, over the condition of the church, which she considered to be inadequately reformed. Her protests carried little weight. Faithfulness to the cause in times of persecution had not won for women a more honoured place in the councils of the church.

CHAPTER 8

OTHER FEMALE ACTIVISTS

Being of the female sex did not turn me from the enterprise of publishing, nor the fact that it be more a manly office ... it is not new or unheard of for women to have such a trade, and one can find many of us who exercise not only the typographical art, but others more difficult and arduous, and who obtain thereby the highest of praise.[1]

By the time Jeanne Giunta of Lyon wrote thus in 1574, female involvement in the printing business, as she said, was not a novelty. This meant not only that women had acquired the necessary technical competence and managerial ability; they were also literate, perhaps in more than one language. In other words, here was a category of women admitted to the networks of scholars and religious propagandists and able, through their control of the means of production, to influence what writings did, and did not, enter the public domain.

When he was arrested in 1535, William Tyndale was working on the translation of the Old Testament. Though he was burned at the stake the following year, his enemies could not destroy the martyr's words. They were printed in Antwerp for a home market eager to obtain the last writings of the martyr. And they were printed by a woman.

Françoise le Rouge was the daughter of a Parisian printer/publisher, Guillaume le Rouge. Sometime before 1517 she married Martin Lempereur, who was probably one of her father's apprentices. When Guillaume died in 1517 the couple took over the business. They must have been among the earliest citizens of the French capital to be won over to the cause of reform, and it was from their presses that some of the earliest humanist and evangelical works came. In 1525 the authorities issued a ban on Bible translation. Rather than abandon their support for the Reformation, Lempereur and his wife moved to the more tolerant city of Antwerp, the hub of the northern European printing industry. Here they published humanist and reformist books in a variety of languages and made a speciality of Bible translations. Despite the liberal atmosphere of Antwerp, Lempereur thought it prudent to change his name to Marten de Keyser. Even then he sometimes used fictitious names on some of his more inflammatory books and pamphlets.

From 1528 onwards de Keyser worked closely with Tyndale (by then living in exile in the English merchants' headquarters) and printed several of his translations and religious apologetic texts. The works of several reformers – English, Flemish, and German – passed through the de Keyser printshop. Here Miles Coverdale, who produced the first complete English Bible, worked as a proofreader for some years. When Marten died in 1536, Françoise continued to run the business.

It must have been an exhilarating time to be part of the print industry. New workshops were springing up in every town and city. Books were still a novelty; they were the smartphones of their day. Just as "cool" customers of the early twenty-first century clamour for the latest communication gizmos, so in-vogue readers 500 years ago were eager to keep up with the latest intellectual trends. It was not just the universities and noble salons that buzzed with novel ideas. Printworks attracted scholars who sought employment as proofreaders or simply hung around to discuss the latest controversial ideas. Women like Françoise de Keyser were party to such debates on an almost daily basis.

Time and again our story takes us back to Strasbourg, and it is there that we find another female publisher/printer. Like Françoise, Margaretha Prüss (d.1542) was the daughter of a printshop owner. She was also a member of the city's religious radical community. She was determined to use her opportunity to disseminate Anabaptist teaching. To do this meant marrying three printers – not simultaneously. The city's printers' guild would not admit women to membership, so when her father died, leaving the business to his widow and her brother, the only way Margaretha could maintain her involvement was by marrying a printer. When he died she married another. And when number two died she sought yet another printer to be her third husband. But her bedfellows were not only guild members; they also belonged to the same radical Christian fellowship. From the Prüss press came a stream of evangelical and radical literature. Margaretha's operation was more a mission than a business. And it was costly. More than once she lost money when the public censors confiscated and destroyed material.

Margaretha's second husband, Johannes Schwann, was an ex-Franciscan who had abandoned his order after a visit to Wittenberg. In 1523 he came to Strasbourg, obtained membership of the printers' guild, and married the proprietress. His reforming zeal coupled with his wife's technical know-how decided the character of the business. Prominence was now given to the writings of Luther but also to those of Andreas Karlstadt and other extremists whom Luther abhorred.

During Margaretha's partnership with her third husband, Balthasar Beck, the press took an even longer stride towards out-and-out radicalism. It published several works by Melchior Hoffman, a self-authenticated proclaimer of apocalyptic, sometimes violent, messages, who travelled throughout northern Europe and Scandinavia, rebaptizing converts and founding churches. In 1533 he appeared in Strasbourg, where he had earlier established a personal following. Now he was prophesying Christ's imminent return and the establishment of Strasbourg as the seat of the New Jerusalem. By now, the patience of the municipal authorities was at an end. Hoffman was thrown into prison, where he died in 1543. By this time the Prüss press had dropped the crazed visionary, but not before a library of works by Hoffman and his associates, including Ursula Jost (see chapter three), had been circulated.

Once again Margaretha and her husband suffered as a result of their support for extremism. As well as the usual confiscation of stock, Beck was summoned to face trial, though he seems to have avoided conviction. It is indicative of the confused state of the times, and particularly in places such as Strasbourg, which adopted an inclusive approach in matters theological, that one of Margaretha's daughters entered a Catholic convent and another married one of the most idiosyncratic religious figures of the day. This was Sebastian Franck, who, when he was not writing or fleeing from persecution, worked in the print trade. His unique theology rejected the tenets of Lutheranism, Zwinglianism, and Anabaptism. He became another radical to achieve the distinction of being outlawed from tolerant Strasbourg.

Throughout the ups and downs of these years Margaretha Prüss was at the side of her husbands and at the centre of the radical element in Strasbourg. There are hints that she may have ventured into print herself, though under male pseudonyms. *A brotherly warning to master Mathis* appeared in 1522–23. It was a tract in the popular dialogue format between a Catholic father and his evangelical son. It was a populist tract which eschewed profound doctrinal debate and was written in a style soon to be superseded by the vitriolic discourse of the 1530s.

Yet another woman printer who used her craft to spread her Christian beliefs was Kunigunde Hergott of Nuremberg. After the death of her husband in 1527, she continued his business. She it was who first published Luther's most famous hymn, "A mighty fortress is our God". The hymnals from her press made no distinction with regard to confessional origins. They contained lyrics by Anabaptist songsters as well as Lutherans.

Arguably the most effective contribution Luther made to the propagation of Protestant thought was involving the laity in the liturgy. Formerly, worship had been performed by the priest, perhaps with the support of a choir, and everything was said or sung in Latin. Luther translated sections of the Mass into the vernacular with parts for the congregation to join in. He also devised his own hymns. He realized that setting doctrine to simple tunes (often borrowed from the pop music of his day) was the best way to get people to absorb evangelical truth. But there was more to it than that. Luther was no mean musician and held music in the highest regard as a gift of God:

> *This precious gift has been bestowed on men alone to remind them that they are created to praise and magnify the Lord. But when natural music is sharpened and polished by art, then one begins to see with amazement the great and perfect wisdom of God in his wonderful work of music...*[2]

Through singing popular hymns laypeople were involved in the life of the church in a new way. It was through hymns that most people, in the early days of the Reformation, became familiar with passages of Scripture. Since this form of expression was not the exclusive preserve of theologians, every layman with a poetic gift might contribute to the growing volume of Christian song. And if not laymen, why not laywomen? It became natural for mothers to teach their children through the medium of sacred song and for women to sing when they came together in the *Frauenzimmer* (see chapter five).

The prize for the first female Protestant hymnodist goes to Elisabeth Cruciger. She was one of the earliest German nuns to leave the cloister. By 1522 she was living in Wittenberg; here she married Casper Cruciger, one of Luther's colleagues in ministry. That was in 1524, which was also the year that Luther's first little hymn book (comprising eight items) was published. Elisabeth as a close friend of the Luther family will have known how much store Martin set by congregational music. She realized that he was eagerly looking for writers of spiritual lyrics. She offered some devotional verses and Luther showed no hesitation in using them in subsequent hymnals. Within a few years they were being translated and used to enhance evangelical worship in other lands. Miles Coverdale, working in exile on an English Bible, also published *Ghostly Psalms and Spiritual Songs*, in which he included Elisabeth's "Lord Christ, God's only Son". There was no question in the 1530s of hymns being sung in the as-yet-unreformed church, so such books must have been designed as aids to private devotion or for singing in small groups. They were, nevertheless, regarded as subversive, and Coverdale's little book was banned. Such "new" music was regarded as a Trojan horse for the infiltration of evangelical doctrine – and rightly so. More scholarly work is yet to be done on early Protestant hymnody, but what is clear is that simple celebration of the mystery of salvation by devout women such as Elisabeth Cruciger was an important means of bringing in evangelical doctrine "under the radar".

Hymns (or perhaps it would be better to use the more-inclusive term "spiritual songs") were highly subjective expressions of faith and experience. Hymn writing was also a "hobby" of Elisabeth of Brandenburg (see above). During her extremely active life she found time for religious poetry, some of which was set to music. Much of what she wrote was commentary on her own adventures and misadventures. The most prolific period of this activity was 1553–55, when she was obliged to live on the charity of the city of Hanover and the support of her family. One of her songs from this period expresses her gratitude to her daughter.

No group of women hymnodists was more prolific than those of the Anabaptist tradition. Persecution, which they regarded as proof of faithfulness, was a fertile seed bed for subjective lyrics extolling heroism, honouring suffering, and denouncing the error of Catholic and mainstream Protestant teachers. Two women of Hall, near Innsbruck, Anna Malerin and Ursula Ochsentreiberlin, who were drowned in 1529, left such a verse testimony:

> ... *Christ brought together his little lambs*
> *And formed a congregation at Mils in the greenwood*
> *But the wolf came running and scattered the lambs:*
> *They ran quickly, crying out to God ...*
> *We will never buy the word of God for money ...*
> *And since they never can succeed they make up many lies.*
> *They say the baptism Jesus ordained is heresy...*
> *And for this reason they shed innocent blood.*[3]

It may have been the association of hymns with the more extreme reformist groups which partly accounted for the slow take-up of congregational singing in the main Protestant churches. While they readily embraced the chanting of psalms in the vernacular, lyrics expressive of personal conviction were regarded with apprehension. In England, for example, it would be more than two centuries before hymn singing took its place as a regular feature in Anglican worship. There were exceptions, however. Elizabeth, Lady Tyrwhitt, was a gentlewoman in the households of three of Henry VIII's queens and, towards the end of her life, in the 1570s, she published *Morning and Evening Prayers*, which included some of the early Lutheran hymn lyrics. In the reign of Elizabeth I (who famously dismissed metrical psalms as "Geneva jigs"), such texts were considered avant-garde.

Most female Christian activists were passive. By that apparent contradiction I mean that they saw their role as being supportive of their menfolk. This was what society expected of them. And not only society. Luther was not the only Bible-loving teacher to point out that Eve was created to be a "helper" to Adam. The emphasis in much of female hymnody – especially Anabaptist hymnody – was on quiet submission to the will of God, even to the point of gladly embracing suffering and death. Yet, again, there were exceptions. The strong apocalyptic strain within Reformation radicalism could express itself in vengeful imagery that was savage in the extreme.

> *At Borsa and Edom, so the author has read,*
> *The Lord is preparing a feast*
> *From the flesh of kings and princes.*
> *Come all you birds,*
> *Gather quickly.*
> *I will feed you the flesh of princes.*
> *As they have done, so shall be done to them.*
> *You servants of the Lord, be of good cheer.*
> *Wash your feet in the blood of the godless.*
> *This shall be the reward for those who robbed us.*[4]

So wrote Anna Jansz of Rotterdam in her song "I can hear the trumpets sounding". Like others who suffered for their faith, she took her cue from Revelation and the promise of vindication for Christ's faithful people.

Not all women, however, were content to wait for the Day of the Lord to witness the discomfort of their enemies. The iconoclastic mobs which appeared in various places, tearing down images and smashing stained-glass windows, were certainly not unisex. An engraving by Lucas Cranach the Elder from the late 1530s depicted a group of women attacking a bishop with agricultural flails and, though it probably did not record an actual event, it indicated the type of protest the "weaker sex" could be driven to, when provoked. In London during the reign of Mary Tudor, the Bishop of London, Edmund Bonner, could scarcely go about the streets without facing angry demonstrations against his fierce persecution of heretics. On one occasion at least he had to order a group of female protesters to disperse. On the other side of the confessional fence, in 1536 a disturbance was caused at Exeter by women armed with shovels and pikes who tried to stop workmen sent by the government to demolish a local abbey.

In the last analysis we are probably wrong to place a dividing line between "active" and "passive" Christians. The possession of vernacular Scriptures and the increasing frequency of sermons engendered among many women a zeal which could not fail to result in action. An Italian visitor in the mid-seventeenth century reported that English womenfolk were "remarkably well-informed of the religion they profess". He noted that they took notes at sermon time. There are many other recorded instances of such assiduousness of women who were keen not only to learn about their faith, but also to pass on what they had learned. Margaret, Lady Hoby (1571–1633), wrote what is the oldest example of an Englishwoman's diary. It contains numerous entries such as "after dinner conferred of the sermon with the gentlewomen that were with me" and "kept company with my friends talking somewhat of the sermon".[5] It is that kind of activity – constant if undramatic – that shaped the character of the nation as much as (and possibly more than) those we think of as "men (and women) of action".

CHAPTER 9

PERSECUTORS – WOMEN AS ENEMIES OF CHANGE

While religious belief can, as we have seen, inspire remarkable acts of courage, endurance, and charity, it can also be used as justification for cruelty and behaviour condemned by all right-thinking people. Sadly, during the Reformation era, the names of some women appear on the roll of persecutors.

England during the middle years of the sixteenth century was unique in experiencing wild fluctuations in its official religion. The monolithic Henry VIII cast off allegiance to Rome and moved his country cautiously in the direction of reform, while always insisting that he remained a Catholic. When he died, in 1547, leaving as his heir a nine-year-old boy, Edward VI, evangelical councillors grabbed the opportunity to establish the realm firmly as a Protestant state with a Calvinist theology, yet retaining some of the trappings of the old faith. Then, in 1553, King Edward died and the throne was taken by his half-sister Mary. She was Spanish on her mother's side and fiercely committed, like her Habsburg relatives, to upholding Catholicism. This see-sawing of religious allegiance plunged the realm into chaos. One result of the queen's determination to turn the clock back was the inauguration of the worst programme of persecution England has ever seen.

To understand Mary we need to go back two generations. The new queen's grandmother, Isabella of Castile, was one of the most formidable women ever to wear a crown. She had to fight for the throne of Castile and, having gained it, she ensured that her husband, Ferdinand II of Aragon, had no authority in her territory; the joint rule they established was unique, each being sovereign in his/her inherited kingdom. To an iron will and a razor-sharp mind Isabella joined a rigid piety. The first major project she and her husband addressed was completing the *Reconqista*, driving the Moors and Jews out of the Iberian peninsula. Although Isabella did not lead her troops in battle, she was revered as a "manly woman" who involved herself closely in the business of war, inspired the troops by her visits to their camp, and sometimes wore armour. The last Moors were driven out of Granada in 1492 but that was only the beginning of what the royal pair had in mind. They were determined that their realm would be *totally* Catholic, God's country, devoid of all trace of other religions and of unorthodox Christianity. The pope conferred on them the title of "Catholic Monarchs" and they did their utmost to live up to their divine calling. One result was the special relationship between church and state which produced the Spanish Inquisition.

Catherine, the youngest daughter of Ferdinand and Isabella, who was married to Henry VIII, inherited her mother's fierce loyalty to her dynasty and her church. It was a great sadness to her that, despite several pregnancies, she produced only one daughter who survived infancy. She was, however, determined that that daughter, Mary, should become Queen of England, maintain a close alliance with Spain, and vigilantly resist the native and foreign pressures to reform the church. When, therefore, Henry began proceedings to annul the marriage, it came as a profound shock to Catherine and she resisted it stubbornly. Whereas most deserted queens would have bowed to the inevitable, she fought for over six years to prevent what she saw as a dishonour to herself, her family, and her religion. But Henry's will was stronger. Nothing would deter him from seeking a new marriage designed to give him the legitimate male heir he craved. The marriage, the Spanish alliance, the authority of the pope, the English monasteries – all went down before him like a row of dominoes.

The bitter contest between her parents was the background against which Princess Mary lived her adolescent years. The annulment of the marriage not only made her a bastard, it excluded her from the succession. Once a coveted prize on the European royal marriage market, she became a political nonentity. But worse than her humiliation was the debasement of everything she held dear. Mary was more than half Spanish; she had been brought up in her mother's household among close personal attendants who came from her mother's country. She was fluent in her mother's language. She thought as her mother thought, believed as her mother believed. To all intents and purposes she was a Spanish princess.

> *Madam, to be plain, as God is my witness …I think you the most obstinate and obdurate woman … that ever was and one that … well deserveth the reward of malice [unless] you be both repentant for your ingratitude and miserable unkindness and ready to do all things that you be bound unto by your duty and allegiance.*[1]

So wrote Thomas Cromwell, King Henry's secretary, when Mary refused to accept the annulment of her parents' marriage and her father's headship of the English church, as decreed by parliament. She was, legally, a traitor and would almost certainly have suffered the ultimate penalty had she not had a last-minute change of heart. What swayed her was the advice of the man she always turned to. This was the pragmatic Eustace Chapuys, ambassador of her cousin, the emperor Charles V. With an eye to the long game, Chapuys counselled her to "dissemble for some time" – i.e. until she might be in a position to reverse the "disastrous" decisions made by her father. Even Chapuys could not have foreseen how events would turn out.

Mary was ecstatic at the death of the young Protestant king, her half-brother, and the warm welcome given her by a populace who hated the late king's advisers. Convinced now of divine favour, Mary pressed ahead with righting all the wrongs of the last twenty years. She married Philip II of Spain and she vowed to Charles V, her father-in-law, "I am content with whatever may be your Majesty's pleasure."[2] She dismantled her father's ecclesiastical legislation. She restored England to papal obedience. She reinstated Catholic worship. She provided military assistance for her husband in his continental campaign. Only two things were needful to make her joy complete: to give birth to a male heir and to deal firmly with the minority of her subjects who clung stubbornly to the reformed faith. In both she was disappointed. She failed to become pregnant and she underestimated the number of English men and women who were as devoted to their beliefs as she was to hers.

The burnings began in February 1555 and they went on and on and on. At least 287 people went to the stake and many more died in prison. As well as these martyrs there were some 800 men and women who fled to the safety of Protestant havens abroad. It was not the most thorough religious purge of the age – Charles V and Philip II sanctioned the martyrdom of thousands of Protestants in the Low Countries – but it was probably the most personal. The changes of the last twenty years had affected her so deeply that she was quite unable to distance herself from the counter-attack against all who had caused her misery and plunged her realm into sacrilegious error (two things inextricably entwined in her mind). She was driven by principle. Unlike her father (and her sister afterwards), she never mastered the political art of pragmatism. Philip and some of his advisers realized that the persecution was proving counter-productive, but either they did not tell the queen or she did not listen.

The policy failed partly because several of the martyrs made a "good end", courageously facing their ordeal and, in many cases, exhorting the onlookers to embrace the evangelical faith. If the burnings turned many people against the regime it was also because they regarded King Philip as an alien imposition. Mary's bishops were seen as examples of Spanish influence. England, it seemed, had become a Habsburg satellite and its people were being milked to pay for Philip's war with France. In Geneva, to which many English exiles had fled, John Knox, contemplating the sorry state of affairs, offered his own explanation of what had gone wrong. His diatribe *The First Blast of the Trumpet Against the Monstrous Regiment* (i.e. rule) *of Women* proposed a simple answer to the collapse of the Reformation in England (and its continuing struggle in Scotland): the people had thrown overboard the divine ordering of society by allowing a woman to rule:

> *We see our country set forth for a prey to foreign nations, we hear [of] the blood of our brethren, the members of Christ Jesus most cruelly to be shed, and the monstrous empire [rule] of a cruel woman ... we know to be the only occasion of all those miseries.*[3]

By the time Knox's book was in wide circulation, Mary Tudor was dead. There can be few sadder spectacles than that of the queen's last months. Ill, denied the child she craved, deserted by her husband, hated by many of her people, in daily fear of assassination, her foreign policy (or, rather, Philip's foreign policy) in tatters, her restoration of Catholicism doomed because her half-sister and successor, Princess Elizabeth, was the product of an evangelical/humanist upbringing, Mary was a prey to melancholia and bewilderment that her God had not allowed her to restore her kingdom to the truth. However, according to a prayer she wrote herself, she took comfort from her own faith:

O Lord Jesu! Which art the health of all men living, and the everlasting life of them which die in faith ... I submit myself wholly unto thy most blessed will ...

Grant me, merciful Father, that when Death has shut up the eyes of my body, yet that the eyes of my soul may still behold and look upon thee: that when death hath taken away the use of my tongue and speech, yet that my heart may cry and say unto thee In manus tuas Domine, commendo spiritum meum; *that is, O Lord, into thy hands I give and commit my soul.*[4]

A few years later, the problems of a nation divided by religion beset France. Catherine de Medici, wife of King Henry II, was as dogged by misfortune as her close contemporary Mary Tudor. She was married to the second son of Francis I but her husband became heir to the throne on the death of his elder brother in 1536. By 1544 the couple had no children and serious consideration was given to Catherine's being repudiated. The marriage was saved by the birth of a son (Francis). Thereafter Catherine bore another five children who survived infancy. Her position and that of the dynasty seemed secure. The first of a series of misfortunes struck in 1559. Henry (King of France since 1547) was killed in a jousting accident. Catherine now became a figure of political consequence as queen mother. After a reign of only seventeen months, Francis II died, and his nine-year-old brother succeeded as Charles IX. Catherine was now in the position of trying to protect her son's independence of action from noble factions determined to direct policy, particularly religious policy.

These years witnessed the rise to power of the Guise family, who were seen as leaders of the Catholic majority. The Calvinist Huguenots looked to Henry of Navarre, the son of Jeanne d'Albret, though their leaders in the field were the Prince de Condé and Admiral Gaspard de Coligny. Sporadic fighting, known as France's Wars of Religion, had devastated the country since 1562. Between then and the end of the century it would claim between 2 million and 4 million lives (out of a population of approximately 19 million). Catherine's overmastering concern was for peace and stability. Many things were against her. The young king was sickly and little interested in government. She was under pressure from the pope and Philip II of Spain to eradicate "heretics". Across France's northern boundary a bitter and ruthless struggle was going on between Philip's agents in the Spanish Netherlands and Calvinist revolutionaries heading a nationalist rebellion. But Catherine's principal obstacle was, arguably, herself. She was a political creature who had little grasp of the deep feelings and theological imperatives which divided sincere French people. She believed that harmony could be achieved through agreements patched up between leaders of the contending parties, but compromise between people holding strong opposing convictions proved impossible.

In August 1572 Catherine's peace plans came to a head with the marriage of her daughter Margaret to Henry of Navarre. This brought members of all the leading families to Paris and provided the opportunity for another element in the queen mother's strategy for stopping the conflict: the elimination of Coligny. He was shot in the street on his way from a council meeting. Exactly who organized this assassination attempt and why has been debated ever since, but most historians are agreed that Catherine was involved. She felt a personal animosity for the admiral and it may be that agreeing to his murder was part of a deal with the Guise faction, who were far from happy about the marriage of the king's sister to a Huguenot.

What was unfortunate about the plot was that it failed. The shot lodged in Coligny's arm and only slightly incapacitated him. Now, it seems, everyone panicked. The Protestant leaders flew to arms, fearing a more general attack. The Catholic leaders flew to arms fearing a Protestant backlash. It was they who struck first. The following morning, armed Guise retainers burst into Coligny's chamber, savagely butchered him, and threw his body from the window. It was the beginning of one of the blackest few days in French history. The St Bartholomew's Day Massacre began in the streets of Paris and spread mob murder throughout the land. An estimated 5,000 Huguenots perished in the national bloodletting.

Neither the king nor his mother can have imagined that the tragedy would go that far. Had they known, they would have realized that the massacre would undermine their credibility. Catherine may have instigated the attack on Coligny or been persuaded into sanctioning it. Either way, her reputation never recovered from the atrocity. Even dedicated royal supporters were sickened. Simon Goulart, a Calvinist minister in Geneva, produced the first detailed account of the holocaust in a three-volume work published between 1576 and 1578. His evaluation of Catherine as an unprincipled politique could not avoid being biased but should certainly not be dismissed:

> among all nations Italy takes the prize for shrewdness and subtlety; and in Italy the prize goes to Tuscany; and in Tuscany to Florence ... When this art of deception falls upon someone who has no conscience ... I leave it to you to imagine the evils that might befall. And, after all, Catherine is of the House of Medici.[5]

The Reformation undermined a political maxim that had hitherto been universally accepted: that every state had to have one official religion – that such a religion was the cement which held the political edifice together. As confessional divisions became commonplace throughout Europe, rulers were faced with a stark choice: toleration or suppression. To tolerate a minority faith was tantamount to admitting that the state church *might*, in some ways, be wrong. How could any king, queen or regent personally committed to Catholicism (and constantly in receipt of harsh missives from Rome) accept such a possibility? That was the difficulty facing a woman like Mary Tudor. For someone like Catherine de Medici, who had a more laid-back attitude in matters of religion, pragmatic compromise might appear to be the way to ensure internal peace, but that laid her open to the charge of not being a faithful daughter of the Church. The secular state still lay centuries in the future. The Reformation confronted rulers with cruel choices. Some responded cruelly.

Elizabeth I of England observed and shrewdly noted the lessons presented by the situation in her own and neighbouring lands. She had, herself, come close to death at the hands of her half-sister. She had survived by keeping a low profile, outwardly conforming to Mary's religion and distancing herself from those who rebelled against or demonstrated disapproval of the Catholic regime. When she came to the throne she applied the lessons she had learned. She famously declined to "open up windows into men's souls" and deplored violence in the name of God. But she, too, could not escape from situations that forced her to become a persecutor.

The young woman who came to the throne in 1558 had shared her schoolroom with her brother, Prince Edward, and their teachers were drawn from the "Cambridge circle" of humanists/evangelicals then greatly in favour with King Henry. She was a very apt pupil and by the age of twelve had mastered

Latin, Greek, French, and Italian. She showed off her linguistic skill in translations of French devotional and theological treatises. At the New Year of 1545 she presented her stepmother, Queen Catherine Parr, with a rendering of Margaret of Navarre's *A Mirror for the Sinful Soul*. The following year her gift took the form of a translation of an extract from Calvin's *Institution of the Christian Religion*. In her letter accompanying the offering Elizabeth described it in glowing terms:

> *... the majesty of the matter surpasses all human eloquence, being privileged and having such force within it that a single sentence has power to ravish, inspire, and give knowledge to the most stupid and ignorant beings alive in what way God wishes to be known, seen, and heard...* [6]

Calvinism would be the theological basis of the brand of Protestantism that Elizabeth adopted for her church. But, while the queen's religion was Genevan in thought, it was not Genevan in spirit. The unique mix of belief and practice which developed as Anglicanism had much to do with the new queen's experiences during her half-sister's reign. She had been interrogated on suspicion of treason and spent two months in the Tower and much longer under house arrest. There had been times when her physical and mental health had buckled under the strain. Self-preservation was uppermost in her mind. When pressed to attend Mass and other Catholic ceremonies, she conformed. But there were events and people beyond her control. Every plot, rebellion or half-baked coup attempt made Elizabeth's position more precarious. They annoyed her, but so did the diatribes reaching England from the Protestant exiles who had fled to the continent. When she came to power she remained wary of extremist or outspoken Protestants. She reposed more trust in those who shared her pragmatism.

Elizabeth faced the same problem as that faced by all contemporary European rulers: how to achieve peace and unity in a country fragmented into religious camps, each convinced that it possessed the truth. This inevitably involved the application of both power and negotiation. In England the balance achieved was unique. The religious settlement was based on government diktat backed by parliament; the people (or, at least, the ones who mattered) were involved in solving the religious issues of the day. The result was compromise. There would be an episcopally controlled church and not one governed by ministers, on the Genevan pattern. The monarch was the head of that church – although, as a sop to those who could not stomach the idea of a woman bearing authority in the church, Elizabeth's title was changed from "Supreme Head" to "Supreme Governor". Worship was to be according to an English Prayer Book substantially the same as that used in Edward VI's day. In order to soften the change, several old long-hallowed rites and ceremonies were sanctioned and reasonable church decoration was declared acceptable. There would be no iconoclastic orgy. Everyone was to attend his/her parish church on pain of paying a fine. This "Elizabethan Settlement" was intended to be inclusive. As long as people went to church and did not make an issue of theological niceties, they might believe what they pleased.

Some of the queen's subjects were not prepared to attend regular Anglican worship and others argued noisily for further reform of doctrine and ritual. On the one hand there were Catholic "recusants" (those who refused to worship according to the Anglican rite). These dissident communities met in country houses to celebrate Mass in secret, led by priests smuggled into the country from seminaries abroad. They looked longingly across the Channel, especially to regimes in Spain and the Low Countries, where Philip II ruled with an iron determination to stamp out all non-Catholic dissent. And, of course, they still owed allegiance to the pope, who, in 1570, excommunicated Elizabeth, thereby absolving them from all loyalty to the crown. This presented many Catholics with an acute dilemma. They considered themselves the queen's faithful subjects but by acknowledging the pope they were technically traitors – aiders and abettors of Philip II's agents who were trying to foment rebellion.

If the Catholic situation was bad in England, it was impossible in Ireland. There religion combined with nationalism and tribalism to render the province ungovernable. In the early years of her reign Elizabeth had hoped to win over the Catholic population "rather by prayer to God than by violent compulsion", but as the years passed, more and more military expeditions were despatched across the Irish Sea. The cost in lives and treasure of the conflict, which continued throughout the reign, was appalling. The effect on the queen was to make her more and more intransigent. Only in the very last days of her life did she abandon her commitment to "violent compulsion".

At home a series of anti-recusancy laws imposed ever-larger fines on Catholics who refused to attend Anglican worship. For much of the time these laws were not rigidly enforced, but as tension with Spain increased and Elizabeth's own advisers urged tougher measures against the "enemy within", she resorted to more drastic action. Troops were despatched to flush out Catholic cells. Priests were hunted down, imprisoned, and, in some cases, executed as traitors.

While all this was going on Elizabeth was also having trouble with her ultra-Protestant subjects, the Puritans, who consistently pressed for further reform. She was increasingly exasperated by both kinds of extremist. "From mine enemy let me defend myself," she once remarked, "but from a pretensed friend, good Lord deliver me." Those "friends" were all around her. Her council, her parliament, the episcopal bench, and the leaders of provincial society included many who wanted to edge her further along the road of reform. In addition to them, there were Protestant leaders abroad who increasingly looked to her for support. A steady stream of religious refugees arrived in English ports and those who stayed at home to fight against Catholic tyranny in France and the Netherlands pressed Elizabeth to don the mantle of Protestant champion. To most observers it was obvious that Europe was involved in a titanic struggle between the forces of truth and error. But not to Elizabeth. She hated the prospect of war for three reasons: it was bloody; it was expensive; and it was politically destabilizing. She believed passionately in the divine nature of kingship. To support rebellion against an anointed head of state was an offence against God. Not only that; encouraging the disobedience of subjects might rebound against her. Only in the 1580s, when war with Spain became inevitable, did she provide military aid to the Dutch freedom fighters.

Inevitably, experience of government in an age of violently competing religious certainties had influenced the queen's own understanding of the faith. She was no longer the little girl who had believed that Calvin's writing perfectly set forth the way "God wishes to be known, seen and heard". However, she could still claim to speak in the name of "the purity of the reformed religion which we profess"[7] when urging the Protestant cantons of Switzerland to go to the aid of Geneva in its struggle with the neighbouring Duchy of Savoy, in 1583. A decade later, when she heard that Henry IV had abandoned his Calvinism as the price of acquiring the crown of France, she gave vent to pious outrage:

Ah, what griefs, O what regrets, O what groanings felt I in my soul at the sound of such news ... My God, is it possible that any worldly respect should efface the terror with which the fear of God threatens us? He who has preserved you many years by His hand – can you imagine that He would permit you to walk alone in your greatest need? Ah, it is dangerous to do evil to make good come out of it ...[8]

That was rather rich coming from a queen who had set her face against the vigorous propagation of Calvinist theology and ecclesiology in her own realm. When groups of clergy and prominent laity met together for Bible study and teaching (called "exercises"), Elizabeth chose to regard them as subversive and ordered the practice to stop. This led to a showdown with her Archbishop of Canterbury, Edmund Grindal. He was not a man to be cowed. Not only did he refuse to obey the royal command, he offered some pointed pastoral advice:

Ye have done many things well, but except ye persevere to the end, ye cannot be blessed. For if ye turn from God, then God will turn away his merciful countenance from you. And what remaineth then to be looked for, but only a terrible expectation of God's judgments, and an heaping up of wrath against the day of wrath?[9]

It was a showdown moment. What was being put to the test was the question "Who bears the rule in Christ's church?" In Elizabeth's eyes, every one of her subjects, including archbishops, owed her unquestioned loyalty. To Grindal, ministers were appointed by God to pastor the laity, including queens, and direct them in the paths of righteousness. Neither adversary blinked. Despite the protests of astonished councillors, the queen sequestered Grindal from all ecclesiastical functions and replaced him with John Whitgift, a man after her own heart. Elizabeth might be a woman but she was a divinely anointed woman determined to bear rule in her church.

Whitgift, an unyielding disciplinarian, went on the offensive against all Puritans who objected to the use of vestments, "popish" ceremonies, and rule by bishops. His purge drew a resentful reaction. A clandestine press published a series of attacks on the status quo entitled the *Marprelate Tracts*. Bishop Richard Hooker, the apostle of the Elizabethan Settlement, boldly asserted, "There is not any man a member of the commonwealth, which is not also of the Church of England."[10] Elizabeth may have believed that this was so and may have been convinced that firm laws and episcopal vigilance could make it a reality. The truth was very different. She left to her successor a kingdom in which significant minorities were clandestinely fed by Catholic priests smuggled in from the continent, or Puritan preachers succoured by books, tracts, and letters from the continent.

Elizabeth's inclination, like Catherine's, was for toleration but, although she never resorted to the same extreme measures as her French contemporary, in the last resort she relied on force – in other words, religious persecution. And for the same reason. Elizabeth required the stability of her realm and the peace of her people. The Reformation, by encouraging men and women to "work out their own salvation with fear and trembling", had rendered this impossible. Political stability and militant prejudice were the upper and nether millstones of state religion, and many were the men and women crushed by them.

CHAPTER 10

VICTIMS

In March 1546, a feisty twenty-six-year-old woman from a good family was brought before Bishop Edmund Bonner of London at his town house to be interrogated on suspicion of holding unorthodox views about the presence of Christ in the Communion bread and wine. Bonner, a corpulent prince of the church in his mid-forties, was a very competent scholar and an experienced diplomat who had represented Henry VIII on several ambassadorial missions. He was also a dedicated heretic-hunter with a reputation for brutality. His confrontation with Anne Askew (1521–1546), a country wife from Lincolnshire, should have been a no-contest. But Bonner was on edge this day, and with good reason. Anne had relatives and friends at the king's court, where conservative and evangelical factions were very delicately balanced. Some of her influential co-religionists had actually come to the bishop's great chamber and were standing in the background to give the prisoner moral support.

The bishop began his interrogation quite gently but, finding Anne aggravatingly pert, he moved to the central issue. Referring to something she had said when examined on a previous occasion, he demanded, "Did you say that after consecration the holy bread in the pyx is still only bread?"

Anne replied that she had been careful not to give a direct answer to that.

"But you did quote certain passages of Scripture in order to refute the doctrine of the Mass," he persisted.

Anne was not to be cowed. "I only quoted St Paul's words to the Athenians in Acts 17: 'God liveth not in temples made with hands'."

Bonner did not appreciate having the Bible quoted at him. "How do you interpret these words?" he asked.

"I believe as the Scripture tells me, my Lord," Anne replied, quietly respectful.

"So, if Scripture says the holy bread is the body of Christ?"

"I believe as the Scripture teaches," Anne repeated.

"And if Scripture says that it is not the body of Christ?"

"I still believe as the Scripture…"

The frustrated bishop interrupted, "Well, what, in your opinion, *does* the Scripture teach?"

The reply came back calmly. "Whatever Christ and his apostles taught, that I believe."

Intent on wringing from her a clear statement of her belief, Bonner asked her to tell him exactly what Christ and the apostles had to say on the subject. This time Anne kept her lips tight shut.

"You have very few words," Bonner taunted.

Anne, seemingly, could not resist a riposte. "My Lord, Solomon says, 'A woman of few words is a gift of God.'"

One can imagine the prisoner's friends trying to hide their smiles. But the bishop was not amused. "Did you or did you not say that the Mass is idolatry?"

"When I was asked whether private Masses relieved departed souls, I answered, 'What idolatry is this, that we should believe more in private Masses, than in the healthsome death of the dear Son of God?'"

Bonner's patience was by now on the edge. "What sort of an answer was that?" he snapped.

"A poor one, my Lord," Anne answered with infuriating calmness, "but good enough for the question."[1]

This verbatim account was written by Anne in prison, smuggled out, and printed by Protestant friends abroad within the year. It is certainly one-sided but must give a reasonably accurate impression of the woman who faced the prospect of martyrdom in the last year of Henry VIII's reign. By the time of her arrest she was well known throughout the capital as a bold, intelligent, and witty controversialist who feared no man.

She was born around 1520, the fifth of six children of Sir William and Lady Elizabeth Askew, and grew up in her father's house, South Kelsey Hall, on the edge of the Lincolnshire fenland. This was regarded as a backward area. Henry VIII dismissed it as "one of the most brute and beastly of the whole realm",[2] but there was nothing unsophisticated about Sir William. Not only was he one of the leaders of county society, he was a habitué of the royal court and occasionally a member of the king's entourage. This meant that he was in touch with the religious and political controversies of the day and that his children grew up in an atmosphere where such things were discussed. Sir William was able to gain a place for one of his sons in the royal bodyguard (the Gentlemen Pensioners) and for another in the household of Archbishop Cranmer. His eldest son, Francis, he sent to Cambridge, one of the earliest hot spots of the New Learning. In addition, which was more unusual in rural society, Sir William had his daughters educated well.

The origin of Anne's "heresies" is not clear. When Bonner pressed her for her understanding of the nature of the Mass and Christ's presence in the consecrated elements he was probably trying to get her to confess herself a sacramentary – someone tainted with Anabaptism who viewed the Lord's Supper as purely a memorial. However, there is no evidence concerning her opinion on this central issue, beyond her insistence that she believed the truth to lie in the Bible rather than the official church.

She would have been able to read the Great Bible, and, perhaps, own her own copy since its publication in 1539 (when Anne was nineteen). She must have learned from her brothers something of the theological matters which were being discussed in academic and court circles. There is nothing in the written records of her persecution to suggest that she had read the works of Luther or any other continental reformer. We know of no group of fellow believers to which she belonged in Lincolnshire. The Bible seems to have been the only source material for her beliefs. What we can say with some confidence is that, having discovered for herself the truth of Holy Scripture, she felt compelled to share it with her friends and family servants. It is easy to imagine her presiding over an English version of the *Frauenzimmer*, where she could bring enlightenment to those unable to read the Bible for themselves.

Anne's problems began with her marriage. The exact timing of events is not clear but what we do know is that Sir William arranged for his eldest daughter, Martha, to marry Thomas Kyme, a farmer of moderate means who lived at Friskney, deep in the fens, some thirty miles from South Kelsey. Like most gentry marriages this was a business arrangement, and, when Martha died before the nuptials, there was no problem about having Anne take her place. The bride began her new life about 1540 in a part of the country deeply set in the old ways. Only four years earlier, the area had risen in rebellion against Henry VIII's religious innovations. Kyme shared the religious conservatism of his neighbours and was spurred on by the local clergy to keep his wife in order. They all underestimated Anne's conviction and fervour. Her gospelling was certainly not appreciated.

In 1543 her opponents were heartened by the passing through parliament of the Act for the Advancement of True Religion. Alarmed by the impact of the open Bible, Henry tried to impose new restrictions. Access to Scripture was forbidden to the lower orders of society – and to all women. Thomas now had the law on his side. If, as seems likely, he took Anne's Bible from her, this must have been the last straw. Anne packed her bags and went back to South Kelsey. Sir William had by now died and it was to the protection of her brother Francis that she appealed. This domestic fracas was the talk of the shire and an embarrassment to both Anne's brother and her husband. Convention demanded that women should be obedient to the head of the family which, in Anne's case, might mean either Francis or Thomas, both of whom wanted her to be submissive. Apparently, that was not a word in her vocabulary. Not even a desire to be reunited with her infant children moved her to compromise her faith. She now desired a divorce and had convinced herself that she had the sanction of Scripture. Had not Paul urged, in 1 Corinthians 7, that Christians wedded to unbelieving spouses were free to break their marriage vows? Well, no. There was more hope than truth in Anne's exegesis. What the apostle adjudged was that a marriage might be dissolved if the non-Christian partner refused to sustain it. The believer's responsibility lay in maintaining the union for as long as possible. But the strong-willed Mrs Kyme was dissuaded neither by argument nor by family pressure. We next find her in Lincoln, where – astonishingly – she went to seek a divorce through the bishop's court.

As might be expected, she was unsuccessful. Still she stuck to her guns. For several days she went into the cathedral, positioned herself beside the chained Great Bible, and challenged any clergy within earshot to engage in debate with her over her case and prove from Scripture that her marriage was still valid in the sight of God. Such eccentric behaviour not only provoked ridicule and anger, it was also dangerous. Anne was liable to prosecution under the Act for the Advancement of True Religion. News of her notorious behaviour spread far and wide. Sympathizers hailed her as a champion of the faith. Critics pointed out that such a public scandal was the inevitable result of making the Bible available to women.

But this persistent woman would not yield an inch. With no one at home to exercise any control over her (Francis had travelled to France with the English army on campaign there), she resolved to go to London, where she could expect support from her other brothers and their evangelical friends. As for her marital case, Anne intended to pursue it in the secular Court of Chancery, perhaps intending to have her marriage dissolved on the basis of Kyme's pre-contract with her sister.

The capital was not a safe place for a lady of unyielding opinions in the winter of 1544–45. Religious conflict was at its height because control of the church was becoming an urgent matter. The king was ill and would almost certainly be succeeded by a minor, Prince Edward. Real power, therefore, would lie with whoever wielded influence in the next reign. More specifically, the dominant faction would determine England's religious future. The turbulent conflict between Catholic and Protestant groups at court sent ripples out into the streets and abbeys of London. Bishop Bonner was alarmed by the growing number of evangelicals. "There are more heretics now than in the last three or four years," he complained.[3] Anne, however, was in her element. Surrounded at last by fellow believers both in the city and the court, she rapidly became a celebrity. Someone called her the "Fair Gospeller" and the appellation stuck. People were obviously struck by both her appearance and her zeal. The term "gospeller" indicated someone who expounded Scripture, usually in small clandestine groups. Presumably Anne ministered in this way to merchants' wives in their town houses, but she also had contacts in the inner circle of Queen Catherine Parr (herself sympathetic to reform).

It was inevitable that she should attract the attention of the Bishop of London. Bonner found her pert and stubborn but, because of her social connections, he took no severe action against her. Having extracted from her a mild form of recantation, he sent this tiresome woman back to her husband with a warning to keep out of harm's way. He was content to discredit Anne (by a public reading of her recantation) and return her to rural obscurity.

But weeks later the religious situation had changed for the worse. The power struggle at court had intensified. The Catholic faction, led by Bishop Gardiner of Winchester and the Lord Chancellor, Thomas Wriothesley, were desperate to implicate their court rivals by association with condemned heretics. It was a tactic that had worked before and now they intended to use it again to bring down the queen and members of her household. Troops were sent to bring Anne back to London. The scheme was to indict her of heresy and force her to implicate her well-placed patrons. They reckoned without Anne's stubbornness. Perhaps by this time she had determined to embrace martyrdom. She refused to deny her own beliefs and to provide the names her tormentors wanted. After her conviction, she was taken to the Tower of London and there put to torture. So desperate were Gardiner and Co. to salvage something valuable from this situation that Wriothesley himself, the Lord Chancellor of England, rolled up his sleeves to work the rack. As far as we know, she was the only Englishwoman ever to be racked. So shocked was the Lieutenant of the Tower that he hurried to court to report to the king and disassociate himself from this illegal act. With incredible fortitude Anne resisted all her tormentors could do. So disjointed were her limbs by the ordeal that she had to be conveyed to Smithfield by cart and fastened to a chair. There she was burned on 16 July 1546, with three other condemned heretics.[4]

Anne Askew may be said to have won her battle. She had cocked a snook at the social and religious conventions, refused to be cowed by the leaders of church and state, and made fun of her accusers. She had given them no alternative but to bring her to the fire. By so doing she had forced them into openly acknowledging that the evangelical movement was getting out of hand and gaining ground among the ruling classes. She had also won a place in the annals of the Reformation as England's most celebrated Protestant martyr.

One problem which did not confront Henry VIII certainly worried the leaders of continental Catholicism. Henry had cheerfully done away with monasticism because it was a Trojan horse of papal authority. However, popes and bishops were also wary of the convents, if for different reasons. They feared that heresy might lurk within the high walls which were supposed to protect the religious from contamination by the world. The number of defections from monasteries and nunneries in Protestant lands was alarming, and Martin Luther was by no means the only ex-religious now wandering at large and calling for sweeping reform. Ironically (though not for the first time), the hierarchy was suspicious of those very elements within the Catholic Church which could have revived its fortunes. The conflict between rigid orthodoxy and religious fervour was not new. There had always been convents which were spiritual hothouses, largely unsupervised by the bishops, where luxuriant mysticism and unconventional expressions of piety could flourish. Moreover, because visionaries, miracle workers, and charismatic preachers tended to be popular with the people, they were even more difficult to control. But now something clearly had to be done and the Vatican went onto the offensive.

In 1542 Paul III issued the bull *Licet ab initio*, which set up the Holy Office to take charge of the war against heresy in all lands and endowed it with almost unlimited powers. From that time the Vatican mounted a vigorous campaign to seek out and destroy all traces of error in convent life. Nowhere were the guardians of orthodoxy more vigilant than in Spain. Supported by the crown, the persecutors carried out their gruesome tasks without fear or favour. Neither rank nor influential connections could protect those upon whom the eagle-eyed inquisitors fixed their gaze.

Doña Marina de Guevara was a lady of noble Castilian birth who had embraced the religious life and, by the age of forty, had become sub-prioress of the convent of Our Lady of Bethlehem in Valladolid. In her ascetic pursuit of greater holiness she was attracted by the teaching of Dr Augustin Cazalla, a scholar and preacher of Jewish extraction and court preacher to the emperor Charles V. Even such a Catholic champion was not immune to the probing of the Inquisition. Their suspicions were aroused when Cazalla, eager to denounce the errors of Luther, got a little too close to the arch-heretic's teaching and began to doubt Catholic orthodoxy. Cazalla was a charismatic figure and when he came to preach at the Valladolid convent, as he did quite regularly, the devout ladies were much attracted to him. A little clique of disciples gathered round him to explore some of the deeper recesses of theology (or, perhaps, just to be close to this exciting and dangerous man), and Doña Marina was a member of this group.

As with the Soviet KGB, the success of the Inquisition rested on creating an atmosphere of fear and employing an army of informers. All lay people were ordered to report any unorthodox activity and were warned that, if they kept silent, they risked sharing the fate of convicted heretics. Sometime in 1557 the trail of innuendo and accusation led to Cazalla. He hastened to send a coded message to Marina advising her to collaborate fully with the Inquisition on the subject of his own preaching but to say nothing about the study group. Marina was on tenterhooks for months, cautiously gathering news of the investigation and waiting for a knock on the door of the convent.

It came on 15 May 1558. She was summoned for questioning. This proved to be only the first of many sessions during which her interrogators became progressively more aggressive and threatening. The devout nun tried to keep the discussion focused on her own spiritual rigours. Many, she said, would testify to her zeal in following the prescribed Catholic penitential routines. But this was not what her interrogators wanted to hear. Like the tormentors of Anne Askew, they demanded names. Which of her sisters and friends did she suspect of being tarred with the Lutheran brush? Marina gave them what they wanted – up to a point. She was careful to specify in her responses only those people who were already in custody or who had fled the country. This temporizing only made her examiners more suspicious. They ordered the sub-prioress to be placed in detention within the convent, pending further inquiries. Then they harangued her colleagues. Time and again the terrified nuns were subjected to private examination and urged to inform against one another. These secluded, other-worldly women, especially the younger ones, were no match for seasoned interrogators whose entire way of thinking was based on the conviction that ends justify means. With the integrity of the Catholic faith and the security of the Catholic hierarchy at stake, they were in no doubt that threats, lies, and mental torture were fully justifiable. And they were well practised at playing on the resentments and jealousies which not infrequently lurk below the surface of community life. Ultimately, it was Marina's tough regimen of personal holiness and zeal in ruling her subordinates which brought about her downfall. It took them little time to obtain from the confused and intimidated nuns sufficient information about Cazalla's group of favourites to proceed to the next stage of their enquiry.

Throughout the humid, enervating summer months, when the temperature exceeded 30°C, the unremitting work of the Inquisition went on. Doña Marina was reduced to a state of complete mental and physical exhaustion. She succumbed to fever and delirium and at one point a priest was summoned to administer the last rites. But the questions and threats of her interrogators were not the worst aspects of her ordeal. She fell prey to agonizing self-doubt. Part of her was ready to die – would actually welcome it. But could she be sure of heaven? She had tried her utmost to gain divine favour. Why, then, had God deserted her? Was Dr Cazalla right to insist that salvation was the reward for faith and not for works? Or had she been diabolically misled by the preacher into forsaking the truth entrusted to the leaders of the Catholic Church? When the fever left her and the examinations recommenced, she tried to retract her earlier statements, insisting that she did not clearly remember exactly what had been discussed in Cazalla's seminars. Her furious examiners warned her of the dire consequences of trying to protect her friends. Then they left her alone for several months. This was a technique of psychological warfare. The forty-three-year-old nun was placed in limbo. Allowed few visitors, she was kept in ignorance of the progress of the investigation. She was left alone to face her inner demons of doubt and despair, in the hope that she would eventually crack and tell the Inquisition tormentors whatever it was they wanted to hear. But this period of prolonged peace had just the opposite effect. Marina's mind cleared. She came to the realization that whatever the Inquisition might do to her was as nothing compared with the damage she could inflict on her immortal soul by denying the truth as she understood it. When the next bout of questioning began, she would adopt a more robust attitude towards her accusers.

It was on 11 February 1559 that she was arrested and taken to the Inquisition prison. Stubbornly refusing to provide her interrogators with clear evidence against Cazalla, she was now accused of heresy and a list of her errors was drawn up. Twenty-four charges were laid against her, including rejection of the doctrine of purgatory, reading Lutheran books, and protecting suspected heretics. Marina denied all these accusations. Her prosecutors, therefore, called for the death penalty to be applied to her. She can have been in no doubt about what that meant, but the grim reality was certainly brought home to her in the spring, when Cazalla and eleven others were burned at the stake in Valladolid's first *auto-da-fé* ("punishment in accordance with the faith"). The victims included other members of Cazalla's family, high-ranking officials, and other prominent citizens. Perhaps most distressing of all for Marina and her community was the action taken against Cazalla's dead mother. Her body was disinterred from its resting place within the convent and publicly burned, along with her funeral effigy. All her family property was seized and her house demolished. It is likely that Marina was taken to witness these appalling scenes, carried out in front of large cheering crowds. In the event, Marina showed more courage than several of the other victims, including Dr Cazalla. They had been prepared to recant their opinions in the hope of escaping the hideous death prescribed by law. The only favour this won them was that of being strangled at the stake prior to being burned. Marina consistently refused to confess to opinions she did not hold and offered the inquisitors no help in discovering exactly what she *did* believe, beyond insisting that she was what she had always been – a good Catholic.

More months passed. Sometimes Marina underwent further examination. At others she was left on her own for weeks. Perhaps the inquisitors hoped for an abject confession. Perhaps, like the obedient servitors of any totalitarian regime, they were simply "doing their job". Ponderously, relentlessly, the clerks of the Inquisition gathered sheaves of depositions from scores of people. They pored over them, compared them, cross-referenced them, filed them. By 27 June the dossier against Sub-prioress Doña Marina de Guevara was complete. She was summoned again and presented with twelve witness statements accusing her of specific heresies. Marina was dumbfounded. She felt sure that other nuns would not have denounced her. She knew that she could not have made some of the doctrinal statements attributed to her – simply because she could not understand them. Any impartial and sensitive tribunal would have understood that they were dealing with the members of a small, introverted community where personal animosities and fear played their part in shaping the evidence they were providing. The Inquisition was neither impartial nor sensitive. At the end of July they gave their verdict. Marina was to be handed over to the secular arm for burning.

It remained only for the decision to be ratified by a higher authority. But here the Valladolid examiners ran into difficulties. The Grand Inquisitor, Fernandez Valdés, Archbishop of Seville, smelled a rat. He was not happy with the progress of Marina's trials and insisted on sending a personal representative to question the prisoner on his behalf. The Valladolid inquisitors were furious at having their competence questioned. In their mindset, opposition – from whatever quarter – could spring only from the enemies of Catholic truth. They confronted their superior and he backed down. He may well have reflected that several princes of the Church had already been crushed beneath the wheels of the Inquisition. Fear lurked in every corner of Spain, including the marbled halls of archbishops.

Marina's death occurred on 8 October 1559 at the second Valladolid *auto-da-fé*. Sixteen other supposed heretics perished with her. King Philip II was present in person to give his blessing to the proceedings. When someone commented on the barbarity of the executions, he gave a reply which has become notorious:

"If my own son were guilty of such crimes, I would, myself, carry the wood for the pyre." The accused had to listen to a long sermon and an even longer recitation of their offences before they were placed on donkeys and taken outside the city walls to where the piles of wood were ready. When it came to Marina's turn, she was strangled before being thrown onto the fire.

But for what doctrine, what heresy, was she murdered? What did she believe, this devout nun who, to the end, considered herself to be a good Catholic? Marina was not academically trained. She lacked the intellectual equipment to read widely and reach firm convictions on thorny matters of theology. That did not mean she was incapable of thought. In her passion to be worthy of salvation she had, inevitably, been ready to listen to anyone who could offer comfort and counsel. Her accusers simply could not see this. To them it was self-evident that the Church offered a "one-size-fits-all" belief system, which must not be questioned. Persecutor and victim confronted each other across a wide gulf. Neither could view the other clearly. When they spoke, their words were distorted by distance. The inquisitors may have believed that they were striving to rescue an errant Christian soul from perdition but they were in no position to know what Marina needed in order to find peace with her God. She tried to point this out; she pleaded with her accusers that their charges were based on misunderstandings and false accusations. Bigots never make good listeners. One of the blackest epochs in European history was under way.

The worst example of mass cruelty, much of it directed against women, was the St Bartholomew's Day Massacre, which began in Paris on 23 August 1572 and swiftly spread across France (see chapter nine). In that city alone, some 2,000 French Protestants (Huguenots) were slaughtered, as crazed mobs, egged on by priests and agents from the royal court, rampaged through the streets crying "Kill! Kill! Kill!" But it was not just mass murder which makes this event even worse than the Terror of 1793. Rape and other violations of women were marked features of this orgy of religious persecution. Madame Le Doux, wife of a Paris artisan, was in labour when the mob reached her house. She was stabbed in the abdomen, and hurled from a window with the baby already protruding from her corpse. Streets away, Françoise Lussault jumped from an upper storey to escape from the men who had already killed her husband. The fall broke both her legs. She was taken in by neighbours but her pursuers discovered her. They cut off her hands to get the bangles off her arms. Her body was impaled on a spit and dragged through the streets before being tossed into the Seine, which was already streaked red with blood.

In England, persecution was sporadic and less virulent. Anne Askew's sad history was one of comparatively few that marred the reign of Henry VIII. He and two of his three children who reigned after him were all committed to the maintenance of a nation united by both obedience to the crown and observance of the official religion, but all were reluctant to use extreme measures to enforce compliance. Unlike contemporary Spanish and French monarchs, they were particularly anxious not to offend the network of noble and gentry families on whose support they depended for control of the shires. The one exception was Mary Tudor (1553–58), whose staunch Catholicism overcame all political and humanitarian considerations. The principal motive for John Foxe's *Acts and Monuments of the Christian Religion* was the putting on record of the almost 200 people executed for their faith during her brief reign. Though his monumental chronicle (2,300 double-column, lavishly illustrated pages) listed martyrs who had suffered in various countries down the ages, it was the English "saints" who interested most of his readers, and their fates helped to forge the anti-Catholic nature of English opinion for four centuries. Seeking examples to illustrate our present theme, we find ourselves spoiled for choice. We will consider just one story: that of Katherine Cawches and her daughters, Guillemine Gilbert and Perotine Massey, residents of Guernsey. In 1556 they were prosecuted for failure to attend Mass. This was not the work of the Inquisition, which was never set up in England, but the events which brought them to their hideous end indicate the existence of a kind of informal Inquisition. During the brief reign of Mary Tudor the government made a determined attempt to stamp out the Protestantism which had been established in the reigns of Mary's father and brother. Agents were sent to detect heretics, and the queen's subjects were encouraged to inform on their neighbours. Despite being supported by several witnesses who testified to their good behaviour, the three women were condemned to be burned. Their execution was one of the most gruesome to be recorded by Foxe.

> *They were first strangled, but the rope brake before they were dead, and so the poor women fell in the fire. Perotine, who was then great with child, did fall on her side, where happened a rueful sight, not only to the eyes of all that there stood, but also to the ears of all true-hearted Christians that shall read this history. For as the belly of the woman burst asunder by the vehemency of the flame, the infant, being a fair man-child, fell into the fire, and eftsoons being taken out of the fire by one W. House, was laid upon the grass. Then was the child had to the provost, and from him to the bailiff, who gave censure that it should be taken back, and cast into the fire, where it was burned with the silly (i.e. holy) mother, grandmother and aunt, very pitiful to behold.[5]*

All these stories of female martyrs point to the opposed world views of Catholics and Protestants in the sixteenth century.

Writing about the persecution of Huguenots, M. P. Holt observed:

> *Viewed by Catholics as threats to the social and political order,*
> *Huguenots not only had to be exterminated – that is, killed –*
> *they also had to be humiliated, dishonoured, and shamed as the*
> *inhuman beasts they were perceived to be. The victims had to be*
> *dehumanized – slaughtered like animals – since they had violated*
> *all the sacred laws of humanity in Catholic culture. Moreover,*
> *death was followed by purification of the places the Huguenots had*
> *profaned ... Many victims were thrown into the Seine, invoking the*
> *purification by water of Catholic baptism.*[6]

Although in numerical terms Protestant regimes were not as dedicated exterminators as their Catholic rivals, they were certainly not reticent about harrying Catholics – even to the point of death. The tragic story of Margaret Clitherow reached its gruesome climax some forty years after that of Anne Askew and is, in some ways, a mirror image of the earlier event.

Margaret too was married to a man who did not share her religious convictions. Despite criticism, she sought the company of fellow believers. She was tortured. She defied her persecutors. She refused to reveal the names of co-religionists. And she was cruelly done to death. The only real difference between the two women was that Margaret was a Catholic.

She was born in York around 1552, lived her life there, and was married there to a prosperous city butcher in 1571. About three years later she converted to Catholicism and her husband, apparently, raised no objection. However, domestic life became strained when Margaret spent short periods in prison for recusancy (refusing to attend Anglican worship) and when she concealed in her house priests sent to teach recusant communities and celebrate Mass.

The background to this activity was an escalating sense of national threat and insecurity. England was in a state of cold war with Spain. The pope had excommunicated Queen Elizabeth, absolving her subjects from their oath of allegiance to their sovereign. Catholic organizations abroad were sending priests and other agents into the country to succour recusant communities and work for the overthrow of the regime. There had been attempts on the queen's life and the government's counter-intelligence agents were kept busy examining plots to displace Elizabeth in favour of the Catholic Mary, Queen of Scots. Although most recusants were loyal subjects, harbouring no treasonous thoughts, the queen's advisers were well aware that, should Philip II of Spain proceed with his long-maturing plans to invade England, many people would make common cause with the foe. Thanks largely to Elizabeth's unwillingness to take drastic action against what her advisers called the "enemy within", there was no consistent witch hunt, but the authorities kept a close eye on known Catholic activists.

By 1586 open war with Spain appeared inevitable and it was in March of that year that a search of the Clitherows' house revealed a secret chamber for concealing a Catholic priest. Margaret was arrested again and this time charged with harbouring enemies of the state. Her response was silence. She would tell her numerous interrogators nothing. Crucially, she refused to enter a plea of "not guilty". Legal procedure at the time established that without a plea there could be no trial. By not allowing her case to come to court she was preventing her accusers from suborning witnesses who would, inevitably, have set the Protestant hounds on the trail of more Catholic activists. However, by her stubborn silence, Margaret was condemning herself, as she well knew, to a hideous fate.

The traditional, if rarely used, form of torture applied to force accused offenders to plead was *peine forte et dure* (hard and forceful punishment). The victim was laid between the ground and a board. Then rocks and other weights were piled on top until pain and the agonizing struggle for breath opened the prisoner's mouth – or closed it for ever. On 25 March Margaret Clitherow was taken to the toll booth on Ouse Bridge and there pressed under possibly seven or eight hundredweight of stones, with a sharp rock under her back. She died either of asphyxia or from broken bones crushing her internal organs. Within fifteen minutes she had achieved the martyrdom she by now craved.

There was one group of Christian believers whom Catholic and Protestant rulers alike regarded as beyond the pale and not protected by any law – Anabaptists. To refer to them as a "group" is actually incorrect, because these radicals espoused a variety of beliefs widely abhorred as heretical. Some were certainly dangerous anarchists, serving an apocalyptic vision which endorsed violence in the establishment of the rule of the saints. The majority, however, were guilty of nothing more disruptive than exclusivity. They sought only to live in their own communities, having as little as possible to do with their neighbours, so as not to be "contaminated" by the world. However, in an age when national unity involved all citizens belonging to church as well as state, this was regarded by all governments as subversive, and many peaceful Christian folk were arrested and forced to recant or be executed.

One radical community, the Mennonites, was founded in the Low Countries by an ex-Catholic priest, Menno Simons. The numbers of these peace-loving people grew steadily. Their fiery ordeal came when Philip II of Spain sent the Duke of Alba to the Low Countries to put an end to both the Netherlandish independence movement and heresy. During his reign of terror, over a thousand men and women were executed for heresy or treason. A century later, the chronicle of those who suffered for their beliefs was written in *The Bloody Theatre or Martyrs' Mirror*, a book which did for the Dutch what Foxe's *Acts and Monuments* did for the English. It included many letters written by the martyrs, which had been cherished by their friends and descendants. One little collection illustrated the fate of Antwerp newlyweds Hans and Janneken van Munstdorp. Hans was burned at the stake in October 1573 but his wife, who was pregnant, had to wait until after her delivery to follow him to martyrdom. She gave birth to a daughter, also named Janneken, who was smuggled out of the prison by Mennonite friends. The distraught prisoner could only leave a letter for the child who would never know her mother:

> *My dear little child, I commend you to the Almighty, great and terrible God, who only is wise, that He will keep you, and let you grow up in His fear, or that He will take you home in your youth, this is my heart's request of the Lord: you who are yet so young, and whom I must leave here in this wicked, evil, perverse world.*
>
> *Since, then the Lord has so ordered and foreordained it, that I must leave you there, and you are here deprived of father and mother, I will commend you to the Lord; let Him do with you according to His holy will. He will govern you, and be a Father to you, so that you shall have no lack here, if you only fear God; for He will be the Father of the orphans and the Protector of the widows.*
>
> *Hence, my dear lamb, I who am imprisoned and bound here for the Lord's sake, can help you in no other way; I had to leave your father for the Lord's sake, and could keep him only a short time. We were permitted to live together only half a year, after which we were apprehended, because we sought salvation of our souls. They took him from me, not knowing my condition, and I had to remain in imprisonment, and see him go before me; and it was a great grief to him, that I had to remain here in prison. And now that I have abided the time, and born you under my heart with great sorrow for nine months, and given birth to you here in prison, in*

great pain, they have taken you from me. Here I lie, expecting death every morning, and shall now soon follow your dear father. And I, your dear mother, write you, my dearest child, something for a remembrance, that you will thereby remember your dear father and your dear mother.

And now, Janneken, my dear lamb, who are yet very little and young, I leave you this letter, together with a gold real, which I had with me in prison, and this I leave you for a perpetual adieu, and for a testament; that you may remember me by it, as also by this letter. Read it, when you have understanding, and keep it as long as you live in remembrance of me and your father. And I herewith bid you adieu, my dear Janneken Munstdorp, and kiss you heartily, my dear lamb, with a perpetual kiss of peace. Follow me and your father, and be not ashamed to confess us before the world, for we were not ashamed to confess our faith before the world, and this adulterous generation.

Let it be your glory, that we did not die for any evil doing, and strive to do likewise, though they should also seek to kill you. And on no account cease to love God above all, for no one can prevent you from fearing God. If you follow that which is good, and seek peace, and ensue it, you shall receive the crown of eternal life; this crown I wish you and the crucified, bleeding, naked, despised, rejected and slain Jesus Christ for your bridegroom.[7]

There was undoubtedly a sexual element to the persecution of women during the Reformation; the nature and brutality of several recorded cases bear ample testimony to that. The new teaching, as well as challenging medieval theology, threatened the stability of society. Access for all to the open Bible encouraged women, as we have seen, to explore their God-given gifts and the possibility of new roles within the church. The prevailing cultures of Western Europe were not hostile to women – as long as they accepted their position within society. That did not restrict them to the roles of wife and mother. They could run farms and businesses, be in charge of convents – even, as we have seen, rule whole nations (as long as there were no males available to do the job). Within the conventions, women were treated no worse than their counterparts in any age. Within the conventions. But if they stepped outside those conventions they became a threat. And that threat unleashed fears which, as the above examples show, ran deep in the male psyche.

If a man fell into heresy, well, that was a sin and the church authorities knew how to deal with it. But a woman heretic was worse. She was condemned not merely for holding erroneous religious opinions but for presuming to hold any religious opinions at all. She had to be subservient to her male guides and protectors – her father, husband, and priest. To set herself up as an interpreter of Scripture, to chop logic with a bishop, to encourage her menfolk in their heresies – in short, to display intellectual independence – was to fall into the sin of Eve, to allow the serpent free rein in Eden – and everyone knew what that had led to.

When women preach and cobblers pray,
The fiends in hell make holiday.[8]

That doggerel appeared in print in 1640, but the anxieties it expressed reached far back in time.

CHAPTER 11

FROM THEN TO NOW

Empowering women isn't about political correctness. It's about improving outcomes. It's about investing in stronger economies and healthier communities. It's about ending conflicts and sustaining peace. It's about improving the quality of life for people all over the world. Empowering women isn't just the right thing; it's the necessary thing. And because women are increasingly ruling, the world is changing for the better.

This analysis was aired by BBC radio in March 2013. The speaker was Dee Dee Myers, former Press Secretary at the White House, and it was backed by, among others, Christine Lagarde of the IMF, Mary Robinson, former President of the Irish Republic, and ex-US Secretary of State Condoleezza Rice. The thrust of the programme was not "if" but "when" the desired transnational matriarchy would come to full flower.

Feminism is on the march. To judge from such manifestos, the age of the New Woman is dawning and millennia of male domination are at an end. Western society has changed. Women have attained political and legal equality and are now achieving equality of function, taking on numerous roles previously reserved (invariably with theological justification) for men. Christians are following this cultural trend, rather than leading it. Indeed, there are vociferous groups within the church which regard this development as a betrayal of "the faith once given to the saints". It is not part of my remit to enter this debate.

What I have tried to do in the preceding pages is to examine that seismic socio-religious phenomenon we call the Reformation and answer two questions: "What did the Reformation do for women?" and "What did women do for the Reformation?" *And yet*, it is not possible totally to ignore our contemporary context. Anyone who writes about the past does so from his/her own specific location in history. An artist looking at objects in a landscape will see them (and represent them) differently according to his/her proximity to them and the angle of his/her viewpoint. So it is with historians. We cannot duck the questions: "Did the Reformation herald a new deal for women or was it a false dawn?"; "Was the closure of nunneries, which provided women with defined roles in medieval society, a retrograde step?"; "Did the re-evaluation of marriage (and noticeably clerical marriage) provide women with enhanced status?" The Council of Trent reaffirmed the traditional teaching that "virginity and celibacy are better and more blessed than the bond of matrimony" (1563). "Did the reformers liberate women from this self-denial, only to 'imprison' them within the home?"; "Did the 'back-to-the-Bible' movement enable women to rediscover their true position within creation?"; "If there is such a thing as 'feminine Christianity', what can we deduce about it from the tangled events, personalities, and doctrinal statements of the Reformation?" The thunder of the sixteenth-century tempest still rumbles on.

Difficult though it may be to offer some tentative answers to such questions, we are faced with a task even more complex. We cannot take 1517 (assuming that to be the beginning of the

Reformation) as our starting point. We can assess the impact of the New Learning only by asking a fresh set of questions: "What did it change?"; "Was the spiritual life of medieval women fully catered for within the institutional church?"; "Were any of them straining at the leash to play more active roles in church life?"; "Were criticisms of convent life justified?"; "How many women were anticipating the Reformation by joining heretical and fringe groups?" History is a continuum and revolutions are simply short periods of time when evolution gets speeded up.

Woman – a woman – *the* woman – lay at the heart of medieval devotion. The Virgin Mary was

a protagonist in the drama of the Incarnation and the Redemption of Christ, and consequently in the personal salvation of each individual who feels himself to belong to Christian history and professes Christian belief.[1]

In the male-dominated world of the Catholic Church there was an acknowledgment of femininity. More than an acknowledgment – Mary, the mediatrix, the eternal mother, the protector, was central to the salvation story. She possessed a unique authority, surpassing that of popes and councils.

Something of Mary's mystic specialness "rubbed off" on various women during the Middle Ages. We might cite the remarkable twelfth-century polymath Hildegard of Bingen – mystic, philosopher, and musician. We could reflect on Catherine of Siena, who, in the late fourteenth century, wandered Italy, calling for reform and challenging the establishment. Most of such female holy exemplars spoke and acted from within the fabric of the institutional church. They were nuns or anchorites. But the mantle of divine spokesperson sometimes fell upon lay women. The mystic Margery Kempe (c.1373–c.1438), famed for her spiritual journal, the first autobiography in the English

language, was a wife and the mother of at least fourteen children.
And then, of course, there was Joan of Arc. Prophetesses, female
visionaries, miracle workers, writers, and protest leaders stand
out in rare but vivid colours from the embroidery of the pre-
Reformation centuries. Though frequently an embarrassment
to their superiors, they (and, after death, their shrines) attracted
crowds of devotees.

There were, yet, other holy women who could not be
contained within the buttressed walls of the official church.
Indeed, one complaint of the establishment about heretical and
fringe movements was their "scandalous" behaviour in allowing
women to exercise leadership or even to preach. Popes and
bishops had good cause to be worried about this phenomenon
because whenever spiritual revival broke out (which they
welcomed), it not infrequently led to expressions of sexual
equality (which they deplored).

The beguinage movement is particularly important to any
understanding of female religious activity before (and, indeed,
during and after) the Reformation. In the twelfth century,
groups of lay women began living together for mutual support
and spiritual encouragement without taking vows or joining
regular religious orders. The word "movement" is, in fact,
inappropriate because there was no overarching organization.
Every community was different both in its activities and in its
beliefs. Some were ultimately absorbed by orthodox convents,
while others drifted into the heretical world of the Cathars. The
social reason for their existence was the superfluity of widowed
and unmarried women in Europe. Some generalizations that can
be made about these amorphous groups, apart from their shared
devotions, include their self-sufficiency through performance of
simple crafts and their neighbourliness. They taught children
and they cared for the sick and infirm. They worshipped and
studied in vernacular languages rather than Latin. This, indeed,

was one factor which raised the ire of the clergy who were always sensitive about movements which "courted popularity" by studying and teaching in the common tongue instead of Latin. When the beguine Margaret de Porete was burned at the stake in 1310, one of the charges against her was that she had published a book, *The Mirror of Simple Souls*, in Old French.

The beguinage phenomenon grew and spread throughout the later Middle Ages and provides ample testimony to the desire of thousands of women to live a life of spiritual observance and charitable service. Though most of them continued to be dutiful daughters of mother church, their simple, practical religion inclined beguines to question the need for a designated priesthood and to regard men and women as spiritual equals.

> *The dogmatic basis for this enhancement of women's religious role was the belief that men and women differed essentially only in terms of their physical bodies, which held no importance in the larger scheme of things. Before God and in heaven, men and women were divine souls and their sexual differences and attendant inequalities nonexistent.*[2]

Medieval religion was a "soup" of many ingredients, including the frustrations and spiritual ambitions of many devout women. It is not difficult to see why Luther's appeal to the Bible (soon to be translated for all to read) over against the papal hierarchy met with such an instant response.

In the first flush of the Reformation, as we have seen, women were "freed" to perform a variety of roles which either were new to them or had previously been performed clandestinely, being disapproved of by the church. They taught, they wrote, they preached, they led worship, they entered into theological controversy, they provided lyrics for public worship and private devotion. Where they were in positions of authority they used their power to further or inhibit the cause of reform. Their contributions were essential to the establishment or eradication of evangelical Christianity in many parts of Europe. The leaders of the new churches welcomed the input of free-thinking women – albeit cautiously and not without some reservations.

The problem was that the key doctrine of justification by faith alone was a social leveller. It implied complete equality in the sight of God. Yet, while it was undoubtedly true that in heaven there was no distinction between male and female, the problem facing the reformers was that God made men and women to inhabit *this* world, and he made them different. They were physically, mentally, and emotionally equipped to perform distinct functions. If the clearing away of Catholic error entailed allowing for the possibility that God was now insinuating women into what had previously been all-male preserves, how were ministers and pastors to distinguish between women with genuine religious callings and presumptuous or mistaken viragos who threatened to upset the divine ordering of society? The mainstream Protestant leaders were grappling with two issues as they formulated their gender theologies and advised their female followers. They wanted to be clear on what the Bible decreed about women. They also wanted to distance themselves from the radicals who, in the name of spiritual freedom, were waging open war on society.

The Peasants' War of 1524–25 came as a terrible shock to Europe. It threatened to overthrow the civilization of the Christian West. Its suppression involved the slaughter of some 100,000 poorly armed insurrectionists. Understandably, critics of reform associated civil unrest with the new theology. Extremist religious leaders on the charismatic fringe of Protestantism, such as Thomas Müntzer and Andreas Bodenstein von Karlstadt, gave credence to such criticism by their encouragement of violent iconoclasm, their demanding of the separation of church and state, their advocacy of "freedom in the Spirit", and their prophesying of the imminent end of the age. The mainstream Protestant leaders were at pains to distance themselves from such apocalyptic extremism and Luther denounced civil unrest and religious protest in some of his more violent writings. Reformers were in the business of changing society, not overthrowing it. Apart from any other consideration, they needed the support of temporal rulers in establishing their own assemblies as official state churches. Thus, before the Reformation was much more than a decade old, the emphasis in teaching and preaching was increasingly on upholding and preserving existing institutions and customs. This affected Protestant attitudes towards women.

Within the ranks of various Anabaptist groups there was recognition of the special gifts given to women – gifts that clearly set them apart as prophets, preachers, teachers, and hymn writers. In the accounts of trials before church courts it is noticeable that such female activists were among the more steadfast upholders of their beliefs. A third of Anabaptist martyrs were women. Some radical cults were very clearly beyond the pale by any standard. The "Dreamers" of Erlangen practised wife swapping, supposedly at the behest of the Holy Spirit. Less extreme groups and individuals also defied law and convention in obedience to the "higher call" of God. The Swiss prophet Margaret Hottinger was one of a group of radical leaders who had taken up teaching roles, not because they were selected by their own community but because they had been "chosen" by the Holy Spirit. Arrested in 1530, Margaret was tried and condemned to be drowned at Ravensburg. When, after an initial ducking, she was lifted from the water and offered a chance to recant, she responded, "Why did you pull me out? The flesh was almost defeated." Whereupon her execution was completed.[3] In Strasbourg, Ursula Jost (see chapter three) regarded the fact that she was called to prophesy as a sign of the imminent end of the world. Agnes Linck was tried more than once for spreading her "heresies" by writing as well as by word of mouth. She was expelled from Solothurn (between Bern and Basel) in 1528 and ordered to desist. She took no notice of this judgment and appeared before the authorities in Basel two years later on similar charges. Like many other defendants, her name disappears from the records, leaving us ignorant of her eventual fate. The sheer number of women like her and Hottinger reveals how big a problem was posed to the authorities by female evangelists whose fervour drove them to reject their "appropriate" station in life. For the radicals, then, "feminine Christianity" was the same as "masculine Christianity"; women could do whatever men could do. This was unacceptable within the mainstream Reformation and, in the course of time, conventional gender roles reasserted themselves even within most Anabaptist communities.

There were, however, a few women who were indisputably in positions of authority – an authority not only recognized by evangelical leaders but welcomed as that of empowering agents who were in a position to spread the gospel. These were the queens, duchesses, and regents who, by accident of birth, inherited thrones or, by accident of death, found themselves ruling in the name of their sons. Free from male domination, do they offer us a clear view of what feminine Christianity looked like in the sixteenth century?

If by "feminine Christianity" we mean those aspects of the faith that express compassion, nurture, gentleness, and quiescence, we might think of Margaret of Navarre or Elizabeth of England as rulers who studiously avoided conflict and, as far as they were able, rejected force as a means of achieving religious unity in their domains. Both queens were clear about the type of Protestantism they espoused but made sure that the doorways to state religion were as wide as possible. "Toleration", to be sure, meant something different to them. Elizabeth's brand, for all her talk of not opening windows into men's souls, was essentially pragmatic, whereas Margaret was passionate about religious freedom and extended her protection to those of different persuasions. To both rulers "religious war" was virtually a contradiction in terms. Despite plots, assassination attempts, excommunication by the pope, and a mini-rebellion, Elizabeth resisted for almost twenty years the appeals of her councillors to take up arms against Catholic Spain or rigorously enforce the law against English papists.

Margaret, no less determinedly, refused to respond to Calvin's protests that she was sitting on the fence. By rejecting confessional labels and winning the respect of humanist, reformist, and traditionalist activists, she maintained a position of influence in an increasingly volatile political environment, which enabled her to encourage the work of reform that was dear to her heart. It was only the hot-headed protest of the Affair of the Placards (1534) that forced supporters of change within the Catholic and Protestant camps to take up uncompromising positions. After the Affair of the Placards France was on a steep downward slope to the Wars of Religion. In the neighbouring Netherlands a succession of female regents declined to enforce to the letter orders from Madrid demanding harsh measures against "heretics".

But any suggestion that international religious wars might have been avoided or the internal peace of states secured if the thrones of Europe had been occupied by women has to take account of the actions of determined, belligerent, and even bigoted rulers such as Isabella of Castile, Mary Tudor, Jeanne d'Albret or Catherine de Medici. In an age when national unity and religious uniformity were regarded as quite inseparable, women rulers could be just as determined as their male counterparts to buttress state churches with judicial authority and military might. Most of them would have believed they had no choice in the matter. All worldly power was derived from one heavenly source. Kings, queens, dukes, and duchesses were vice-regents, responsible to God for the stability of their territories and the well-being of their people. Theirs was a solemn – even a holy – responsibility. The religious truth to which they subscribed – whether Catholic, Lutheran or Calvinist – they were obliged in all conscience to propagate among their subjects. When the emperor Charles V was forced to come to terms with the Lutheran princes of his empire, the basis of their religious compromise was *cuius region eius religio* ("The ruler's faith is the faith of his people"). This purely political solution struck at the heart of the gospel, which insists that every individual is responsible for responding to the saving grace of God. It would take more than 300 years for that freedom to be written into the constitutions of European states. For the time being, Christian truth had to bow to political stability. Some female rulers found this hard to accept. Some did not.

The vast majority of women were neither rulers nor marginalized radicals. As we have seen, those possessed of a lively faith sought to express their devotion and exert a Christian influence according to the opportunities provided by their talents and their social status. Their lives make up a rich and extremely varied picture of sixteenth- and seventeenth-century life, rather like the crowded tapestries that covered the walls of the wealthy. Only in recent decades has the light of scholarship been directed at these vivid narrative panels, too long ignored in the telling and retelling of the activities of politicians, preachers, and theologians.

Some writers bewail the fact that, in the fullness of time, the prevailing social order reasserted itself, leaving "contemporary women only bit parts in the man's world outside the home".[4] Certainly, after the initial froth and bubble of the Reformation had died down, most of the audacious experiments in female religious activity were abandoned. Christians are always involved in relating the message of the Bible to the age in which they live. It is, therefore, not surprising that things possible between 1520 and 1560 were unacceptable in subsequent years.

That does not mean that the gains made by women during the Reformation were, thereafter, "lost", or that the impact of feminine Christianity on society had no staying power. For one thing, the stories of hundreds of remarkable women remain in the record, ready to be rediscovered as sources of inspiration for modern Christians – men as well as women. For another, the convictions of Reformation women have resurfaced over and over again to inspire their spiritual descendants and challenge the leaders of society. In 1649 a body of women protested to the Long Parliament that their concerns were not being heard:

Since we are assured of our Creation in the image of God,
and of an interest in Christianity, equal unto men, as also of
a proportionable share in the Freedom of this Commonwealth,
we cannot help but wonder and grieve that we should appear so
despicable in your eyes as to be thought unworthy to petition or
present our grievances to this honourable House.[5]

More fundamental, however, is the fact that the Reformation *did* effect one monumental and enduring change in Western society. And this takes us right back to the beginning of our story – the marriage of the monk Martin Luther to the ex-nun Catherine von Bora. This was both a challenge to Catholic teaching on the virtue of virginity and clerical celibacy and an assertion of Bible truth about God's purposes in creation. Luther, it seems, never tired of writing and preaching on this subject and it formed an important part of his pastoral oversight. It was towards the end of his life (in August 1545) that he addressed the female members of his congregation, urging them to think highly of their estate and reflect on it positively in prayer:

> *I thank God that I have been created a woman, and that we have been placed by God in the holy estate of matrimony in order to raise children in accord with his blessing and will. That is a great glory that married people have. For that reason no-one should hate or condemn the estate and ordinance of God ... It is sufficient for us to know that God sees us together with his only Son, our Lord Jesus Christ, who sits at the right hand of God and is Lord of all, as he ordained the wedded estate, set us in it, and presides over it until the Last Day.*[6]

From this time on marriage was honoured within the Protestant tradition as the norm for most of humankind. It was the fundamental building block of society, and at the heart of most communities there was a pastoring couple. If wives were the junior members of these partnerships, their position was in no wise inferior. Their role as "helpmeet" involved the fundamental tasks of rearing and teaching children, managing their households, and exercising Christian neighbourliness.

Over the subsequent centuries the options available to women have increased far beyond what either Dr Luther or Mrs Luther could ever have envisaged. Western society has changed. It is no longer hierarchical. It understands "freedom" as something very different from what the word implied in the sixteenth century. Yet in the worldwide church, opinion is still divided (as it was 500 years ago) on the place of women in the household of faith – witness the differences in attitude (sometimes violently expressed) towards the ordination of women as ministers and bishops. Yet a more fundamental realignment of gender roles has overtaken the lives of husbands and wives. In the interests of raising living standards and achieving greater self-fulfilment, breadwinning and nurture have become shared responsibilities. And then there is the issue of the "nuclear family". Is it, or is it not, a divine institution, which Christians are pledged to maintain? Believers still have to make adjustments, have to square their responses to contemporary culture with the demands of God as recorded in Holy Scripture. Weighing individual prosperity and self-improvement in the balance against the church's patterning of God's plan for human society is a constant challenge. It confronted our spiritual ancestors and ancestresses during the Reformation. So, as we face it, we may find some enlightenment in the lives and witness of Mrs Luther and her sisters.

NOTES

CHAPTER 1: Dr and Mrs Luther

1. H. Bornkamm, *Luther in Mid-Career*, Philadelphia, PA: Fortress Press, page 409.
2. Cf. R. Bainton, *Here I Stand: A Life of Martin Luther*, Oxford: Basil Blackwell, 1987, page 288.
3. *Luther's Works*, (eds) H. T. Lehmann and J. Pelikan (hereafter cited as "*LW*"), St Louis and Philadelphia: Concordia Publishing House, 1955–1936, Vol. 7, page 172.
4. *LW*, Vol. 49, page 117.
5. Ibid., page 276.
6. M. Brecht, *Martin Luther – The Preservation of the Church, 1532–1546*, Philadelphia, PA: Fortress Press, page 243.
7. Ibid.
8. H. A. Oberman, *Luther: Man Between God and the Devil*, New Haven, CT: Yale University Press, page 280.
9. S. C. Karant-Nunn and M. E. Wiesner-Hanks, *Luther on Women – A Sourcebook*, Cambridge: CUP, 2003, pages 187–88.
10. Ibid., pages 28–29.
11. Ibid., page 197.
12. Ibid., page 28.
13. Ibid., page 190.
14. R. Bainton, op. cit., page 293.
15. *LW*, Vol. 54, page 422.
16. S. C. Karant-Nunn and M. E. Wiesner-Hanks, op. cit., page 194.
17. *LW*, Vol. 50, page 294.
18. J. C. Smith, "Katherine von Bora through Five Centuries: A Historiography" in *Sixteenth Century Journal* 30, 1999, Appendix, Letter C.

CHAPTER 2: Wives and Mothers

1. D. MacCulloch, *Reformation: Europe's House Divided, 1490–1700*, London: Penguin, 2003, page 182.

2. E. A. McKee, *Katherine Schütz Zell: Church Mother*, Chicago, 2006, quoted in
   K. Stjerna, *Women and the Reformation*, Malden, MA/Oxford: Blackwell, 2009,
   page 126.

3. "Entschuldigung Katharina Schützinn", quoted in R. Bainton, *Women
   of the Reformation: In Germany and Italy*, Minneapolis, MN: Augsburg, 1971,
   page 75.

4. E. A. McKee, op. cit., cf. K. Stjerna, op. cit., page 126.

5. R. Bainton, op. cit., page 65.

6. K. Head, "Marie Dentière – A Propagandist for the Reform", in
   K. M. Wilson (ed.), *Women Writers of the Renaissance and Reformation*, Athens,
   GA: University of Georgia Press, 1987, page 260.

7. Cf. P. Collinson, *Godly People: Essays on English Protestantism and Puritanism*,
   London: Hambledon Press, 1983, page 285.

8. Cf. J. N. King, "John Day, master printer of the English Reformation"
   in P. Marshall and A. Ryrie (eds), *The Beginnings of English Protestantism*,
   Cambridge: CUP, 2002, pages 185–89.

9. Calendar of State Papers Foreign, 1547–53.

10. C. Goff, *A Woman of the Tudor Age*, London: Murray, 1930, page 188.

11. State Papers Domestic of the Reign of Elizabeth, III. 9.

12. Lambeth Palace Library, MS 651, fol. 156.

13. Ibid., MS 650, fol. 228.

14. J. Spedding, *The Life and the Letters of Francis Bacon* ... London: Longman,
    Green, Longman and Roberts, 1861, pages 110–111.

CHAPTER 3: Women in Community

1. P. A. MacKenzie (trans.), *Caritas Pirckheimer – A Journal of the Reformation Years
   1524–1528*, Cambridge: D. S. Brewer, 2006, pages 19–21.

2. D. MacCulloch, *Reformation – Europe's House Divided 1490–1700*, 2003, pages
   214–15.

3. Ibid., page 30.

4. P. R. Baernstein, *A Convent Tale – A Century of Sisterhood in Spanish Milan*, New
   York: Routledge, 2002, page 58.

5. Ibid., page 63.

6. C. A. Snyder and L. A. H. Hecht, *Profiles of Anabaptist Women – Sixteenth-
   Century Reforming Pioneers*, Waterloo, Canada: Wilfrid Laurier University Press,
   1996, page 282.

7. P. A. Mackenzie, op. cit., page 20.

8. M. Wiesner-Hanks (ed.), *Converts Confront the Reformation: Catholic and
   Protestant Nuns in Germany*, Milwaukee, WI: Marquette University Press,
   1996, page 29.

CHAPTER 4: Women in Power

1. *Selected Writings of John Knox: Public Epistles, Treatises and Expositions to the year 1559*, Dallas, TX: Presbyterian Heritage Publication, 1995, pages 145–46.

2. K. Zimmermann (ed.), *Luther's Letters to Women*, London: Chapman and Hall, 1865, 2.21.

3. R. H. Bainton, *Women of the Reformation: In Germany and Italy*, 1971, page 120.

4. R. Bainton, op. cit., page 131.

5. Ibid., page 141.

6. Cf. R. Bainton, *Women of the Reformation: In France and England*, Minneapolis, MN: Augsburg, 2007, page 21.

7. Margaret of Navarre, *The Mirror of the Sinful Soul*, translated by Princess Elizabeth, London: Asher, 1897, page 141.

8. A. Brundin, *Vittoria Colonna and the Spiritual Poetics of the Italian Reformation*, Cambridge: Ashgate, 2008, page 103.

9. B. Collett, "The Long and Troubled Pilgrimage: A Reading of Marguerite de Navarre's Poetry, 1540–1545", *Studies in Reformed Theology and History* (6), Princeton, 2000, Appendix B, Cf. K. Stjerna, op. cit., page 155.

10. N. L. Roelker, *Queen of Navarre: Jeanne d'Albret*, Cambridge, MA: Belknap Press of Harvard University, 1968, page 142.

11. R. Bainton, *Women of the Reformation: In France and England*, 2007, page 67.

12. Ibid., page 190.

13. S. Carroll, *Martyrs and Murderers – The Guise Family and the Making of Europe*, Oxford: OUP, 2009, page 12.

14. R. Bainton, op. cit., page 249.

15. Cf. K. Stjerna, op. cit., page 194.

16. J. F. A. Dawson, "The Two John Knoxes: England, Scotland and the 1558 tracts", in *The Journal of Ecclesiastical History*, 1991, page 557.

17. P. E. Ritchie, *Mary of Guise in Scotland 1548–1560: A Political Career*, East Linton: Tuckwell, 2002, page 210.

CHAPTER 5: The Educated Woman

1. D. Robin, "Cassandra Fedele (1465–1558)" in R. Russell (ed.), *Italian Women Writers: A Bio-Bibliographical Source Book*, Westport, CT: Greenwood Press, 1994, page 162.

2. D. Robin (ed.), *Laura Cereta: Collected Letters of a Renaissance Feminist*, Chicago: University of Chicago Press, 1997, page 78.

3. Cf. R. Bainton, *Women of the Reformation: In Germany and Italy*, 1971, page 202.

4. K. Benrath (trans. H. Zimmern), *Bernardino Ochino of Siena – A Contribution Towards the History of the Reformation*, London: J. Nisbet & Co., 1876, page 75.

5. Cf. R. Bainton, *Women of the Reformation: In Germany and Italy*, 2007, pages 204–05.

6. Ibid., page 206.

7. *Collected Works of Erasmus – Colloques*, Toronto/Buffalo/London, 1997, pages 502–03.

8. R. H. Bainton, op. cit., page 141.

9. M. C. Erler, "Thomas Cromwell's Abbess, Margaret Vernon", in *History Today*, February 2014, pages 23f.

10. C. B. Brown, *Singing the Gospel – Lutheran Hymns and the Success of the Reformation*, Cambridge, MA: Harvard University Press, 2005, page 162.

11. Ibid., page 117.

12. Ibid., page 165.

13. Cf. K. E. Kvam, L. S. Schearing and V. H. Ziegler, *Eve and Adam: Jewish, Christian and Muslim Readings on Genesis and Gender*, Bloomington, IN: University of Indiana Press, 1999, pages 251–52.

14. *Luther's Works*, (1967) 40, page 391.

CHAPTER 6: Women Venturing into Print

1. Cf. K. Stjerna, *Women and the Reformation*, 2009, page 135.

2. R.H. Bainton, *Women of the Reformation: In Germany and Italy*, 2007, pages 98–100.

3. Ibid., page 97.

4. Ibid., pages 105–06.

5. E. A. McKee, *Katharina Schütz Zell, Church Mother: The Writings of a Protestant Reformer in Sixteenth-Century Germany*, Chicago: University of Chicago Press, 2006, page 64.

6. C. A. Snyder and L. A. H. Hecht, *Profiles of Anabaptist Women: Sixteenth-Century Reforming Pioneers*, 1996, page 282.

7. Ibid., pages 283–84.

8. R. Marius, *Martin Luther – The Christian between God and Death*, Cambridge, MA: Belknap Press of Harvard University, 1999, page 440.

9. K. M. Wilson (ed.), *Women Writers of the Renaissance and Reformation*, 1987, pages 270–71.

10. Ibid., pages 277–78.

11. S. R. Catley (ed.), *The Acts and Monuments of John Foxe*, London: R. B. Seeley and W. Burnside, 1838, V, pages 555f.

12. *Katherine Parr: Complete Works and Correspondence*, J. Mueller (ed.), Chicago: University of Chicago Press, 2011, page 458.

13. Ibid., pages 458–59.

14. H. N. Parker, *Olympia Fulvia Morata 1536–1555; The Complete Writings of an Italian Heretic*, Chicago: University of Chicago Press, 2003, page 179.

15. R. Bainton, op. cit., page 259.

16. Cf. K. Stjerna, *Women and the Reformation*, 2009, page 206.

17. Ibid., page 204.

18. R. Bainton, op. cit., page 261.

19. Ibid., pages 264–66.

20. K. Stjerna, op. cit., page 207.

CHAPTER 7: Patrons and Protégés

1. R.H. Bainton, op. cit., page 195.

2. D. MacCulloch, *Reformation – Europe's House Divided 1490–1700*, 2003, pages 214–15.

3. Cf. P. Schaff, *History of the Christian Church, VIII*, New York: Charles Scribner, 1960, page 162.

4. R. Bainton, op. cit., page 229.

5. M. F. Harkrider, *Women, Reform and Community in Early Modern England*, Woodbridge: The Boydell Press, 2008, page 67.

CHAPTER 8: Other Female Activists

1. Cf. N. Z. Davis, "Women in the crafts in sixteenth-century Lyon", in *Feminist Studies 8*, 1982, page 47.

2. R. Bainton, *Here I Stand*, 1987, page 343.

3. C. A. Snyder and L. A. H. Hecht (eds), *Profiles of Anabaptist Women*, 1996, page 192.

4. Ibid., page 340.

5. Cf. K. Charlton, *Women, Religion and Education in Early Modern England*, London: Routledge, 1999, pages 158–59.

CHAPTER 9: Persecutors – Women as Enemies of Change

1. T. Hearne, *Sylloge Epistolarum*, Oxford: Athens, 1716, pages 137–38.

2. *Calendar of State Papers Spanish XIII*, 228.

3. *The Selected Writings of John Knox ...*, 1995, Preface.

4. J. Strype, *Ecclesiastical Memorials*, Oxford: Clarendon Press, 1816, III, ii, page 550.

5. S. Goulart, *Mémoires de l'état de France Charles IX, 1578*, Vol. III, Middelburg, page 422.

6. L. S. Marcus, J. Mueller and M. B. Rose (eds), *Elizabeth I: Collected Works*, Chicago: University of Chicago Press, 2000, page 12.

7. H. Robinson, *The Zurich Letters*, 2nd Series, 1845, page 319.

8. L. S. Marcus, J. Mueller and M. B. Rose (eds), op. cit., pages 370–71.

9. Cf. P. Collinson, *Archbishop Grindal 1519–1583*, Berkley: University of California Press, 1979, page 245.

10. R. Hooker, *Of the Laws of Ecclesiastical Polity*, Cambridge, MA: The Belknap Press of Harvard University, 1981, Bk VIII, page 130.

CHAPTER 10: Victims

1. H. Christmas (ed.), *Select Works of John Bale*, Cambridge: CUP, 1849, pages 154 ff.

2. State Papers of Henry VIII, 1836, I, page 463.

3. Letters and Papers Foreign and Domestic of the Reign of Henry VIII, 1862–1910, xxi, pt. i, page 836.

4. H. Christmas (ed.), *Select Works of J. Bale*, 1849; G. Townsend and S. R. Catley (eds), John Foxe, *Acts and Monuments of the Christian Religion*, 1838, V, page 537ff.; D. Wilson, *A Tudor Tapestry: Men, Women and Society in Reformation England*, Pittsburgh, PA: University of Pittsburgh Press, 1972.

5. John Foxe, op. cit., VIII, pages 229–230.

6. M. P. Holt, *The French Wars of Religion, 1562–1629*, Cambridge: CUP, 2005, page 87.

7. H. Hillerbrand, *The Protestant Reformation*, New York: Harper Collins, 1968, pages 146–52.

8. J. Taylor, *Lucifer's Lackey*, 1640.

CHAPTER 11: From Then to Now

1. H. Warner, *Alone of All Her Sex – The Myth and the Cult of the Virgin Mary*, Oxford: OUP, 1976, page xxiii.

2. S. Ozment, *The Age of Reform 1250–1550*, New Haven, CT: Yale University Press, 1969, page 92.

3. C. A. Snyder and L. A. H. Hecht (eds), *Profiles of Anabaptist Women*, Waterloo, Canada: Wilfrid Laurier University Press, 2008, page 52.

4. S. Ozment, *Ancestors: The Loving Family in Old Europe*, Cambridge, MA: Harvard University Press, 2001, page 31.

5. Cf. E. A. McArthur, "Women Petitioners and the Long Parliament", *English Historical Review 24* (1909), page 708.

6. Cf. S. C. Karant-Nunn and M. E. Wiesner-Hanks, *Luther on Women – A Sourcebook*, 2003, page 98.

BIBLIOGRAPHY

Aram, B., *Juana the Mad – Sovereignty and Dynasty in Renaissance Europe*, Baltimore, MD: Johns Hopkins University Press, 2005.

Baernstein, P. R., *A Convent Tale – A Century of Sisterhood in Spanish Milan*, New York: Routledge, 2002.

Bainton, R., *Here I Stand: A Life of Martin Luther*, Oxford: Basil Blackwell, 1987.

Bainton, R., *Women of the Reformation: From Spain to Scandinavia*, Minneapolis, MN: Augsburg, 1977.

Bainton, R., *Women of the Reformation: In France and England*, Minneapolis, MN: Augsburg, 1973.

Bainton, R., *Women of the Reformation: In Germany and Italy*, Minneapolis, MN: Augsburg, 1971.

Benrath, K. (trans. H. Zimmern), *Bernardino Ochino of Siena – A Contribution Towards the History of the Reformation*, London: J. Nisbet & Co., 1876.

Bornkamm, H., *Luther in Mid-Career, 1521–1530* (trans. E. T. Barkmann), Philadelphia, PA: Fortress Press, 1983.

Brecht, M., *Martin Luther – The Preservation of the Church, 1532–1546*, Philadelphia, PA: Fortress Press, 1999.

Brown, C. B., *Singing the Gospel – Lutheran Hymns and the Success of the Reformation*, Cambridge, MA: Harvard University Press, 2005.

Brundin, A., *Vittoria Colonna and the Spiritual Poetics of the Italian Reformation*, Cambridge: Ashgate, 2008.

Calendar of State Papers Foreign, 1547–53, 1863–1950.

Calendar of State Papers Spanish, 1892–99.

Caritas Pirckheimer – A Journal of the Reformation Years 1524–1528 (trans. P.A. MacKenzie), Cambridge: Boydell & Brewer Ltd, 2006.

Carroll, S., *Martyrs and Murderers – The Guise Family and the Making of Europe*, Oxford: OUP, 2009.

Catley, S. R. (ed.), *The Acts and Monuments of John Foxe*, London: R. B. Seeley and W. Burnside, 1838.

Charlton, K., *Women, Religion and Education in Early Modern England*, London: Routledge, 1999.

Christmas, H. (ed.), *Select Works of John Bale*, Cambridge: CUP, 1849.

Collected Works of Erasmus – Colloques, Toronto/Buffalo/London, 1997.

Collett, B., *The Long and Troubled Pilgrimage: A Reading of Marguerite de Navarre's Poetry, 1540–1545*, Studies in Reformed Theology and History (6), Princeton, 2000.

Collinson, P., *Godly People: Essays on English Protestantism and Puritanism*, London: Hambledon Press, 1983.

Collinson, P., *Archbishop Grindal 1519–1583*, Berkley, CA: University of California Press, 1979.

Davis, N. Z., "Women in the crafts in sixteenth-century Lyon", in *Feminist Studies* (8), 1982.

Dawson, J. F. A, "The Two John Knoxes: England, Scotland and the 1558 tracts", in *The Journal of Ecclesiastical History*, 1991.

Erler, M. C., "Thomas Cromwell's Abbess, Margaret Vernon", in *History Today*, February 2014.

Goff, C., *A Woman of the Tudor Age*, London: Murray, 1930.

Goulart, S., *Mémoires de l'estat de France sous Charles IX*, Vol. III, Middelburg, 1578.

Guy, J., *A Daughter's Love – Thomas and Margaret More*, London: Harper Perennial, 2008.

Harkrider, M. F., *Women, Reform and Community in Early Modern England*, Woodbridge: The Boydell Press, 2008.

Head, K., "Marie Dentière – A Propagandist for the Reform", in K. M. Wilson (ed.), *Women Writers of the Renaissance and Reformation*, Atlanta, GA: University of Georgia Press, 1987.

Hearne, T., *Sylloge Epistolarum*, Oxford, 1716.

Hillerbrand, H., *The Protestant Reformation*, New York: Harper Collins, 1968.

Holt, M. P., *The French Wars of Religion, 1562–1629*, Cambridge: CUP, 2005.

Hooker, R., *Of the Laws of Ecclesiastical Polity*, Bk VIII, Cambridge, MA: The Belknap Press of Harvard University, 1981.

Karant-Nunn, S. C. and Wiesner-Hanks, M .E., *Luther on Women – A Sourcebook*, Cambridge: CUP, 2003.

King, J. N., "John Day, master printer of the English Reformation", in P. Marshall and A. Ryrie (eds), *The Beginnings of English Protestantism*, Cambridge: CUP, 2002.

Knox, John, *Selected Writings: Public Epistles, Treatises and Expositions to the year 1559*, Dallas, TX: Presbyterian Publications, 1995.

Kvam, K. E., Schearing, L. S., and Ziegler, V. H., *Eve and Adam: Jewish, Christian and Muslim Readings on Genesis and Gender*, Bloomington, IN: Indiana University Press, 1999.

Lambeth Palace Library, MS 651, fol. 156.

Luther's Works, (ed.) Lehmann, H. T. and Pelikan, J., St Louis and Philadelphia: Concordia Publishing House, 1955–1986.

MacCulloch, D., *Reformation: Europe's House Divided, 1490–1700*, London: Penguin, 2003.

Mahoney, I., *Madame Catherine: The Life of Catherine de Medici*, Littlehampton Book Services Ltd, 1976.

Margaret of Navarre, *The Mirror of the Sinful Soul, translated by Princess Elizabeth*, London: Asher, 1897.

Marcus, L. S., Mueller, J., and Rose, M. B. (eds), *Elizabeth I: Collected Works*, Chicago, IL: University of Chicago Press, 2000.

Marius, R., *Martin Luther – The Christian between God and Death*, Cambridge, MA: Belknap Press of Harvard University, 1999.

McArthur, E. A., "Women Petitioners and the Long Parliament", *English Historical Review 24*, (1909).

McKee, E. A., *Katharina Schütz Zell, Church Mother, The Writings of a Protestant Reformer in Sixteenth-Century Germany*, Chicago, IL: University of Chicago Press, 2006.

Mueller, J. (ed.), *Katherine Parr: Complete Works and Correspondence*, Chicago, IL: University of Chicago Press, 2011.

Oberman, H. A., *Luther: Man between God and the Devil*, New Haven, CT: Yale University Press, 1989.

Ozment, S., *Ancestors, The Loving Family in Old Europe*, Cambridge, MA: Harvard University Press, 2001.

Ozment, S., *The Age of Reform 1250–1550*, New Haven, CT: Yale University Press, 1969.

Parker, H. N., *Olympia Fulvia Morata 1536–1555; The Complete Writings of an Italian Heretic*, Chicago, IL: University of Chicago Press, 2003.

Ritchie, P. E., *Mary of Guise in Scotland 1548–1560: A Political Career*, East Linton: Tuckwell Press, 2002.

Robin, D. (ed.), *Laura Cereta: Collected Letters of a Renaissance Feminist*, Chicago, IL: University of Chicago Press, 1997.

Robin, D., "Cassandra Fedele (1465–1558)", in R. Russell (ed.), *Italian Women Writers: A Bio-Bibliographical Source Book*, Westport, CT: Greenwood Press, 1994.

Robinson, H., *The Zurich Letters*, Parker Society 2nd Series, Cambridge: CUP, 1845.

Roelker, N. L., *Queen of Navarre: Jeanne d'Albret*, Cambridge, MA: The Belknap Press of Harvard University Press, 1968.

Schaff, P., *History of the Christian Church VIII*, New York: Charles Scribner, 1859.

Smith, J. C., "Katherine von Bora Through Five Centuries: A Historiography", in *Sixteenth Century Journal 30*, 1999.

Snyder, C. A. and Hecht, L. A. H., *Profiles of Anabaptist Women: Sixteenth-Century Reforming Pioneers*, Waterloo, Canada: Wilfrid Laurier University Press, 1996.

Spedding, J., *The Life and the Letters of Francis Bacon …* , London: Longman, Green, Longman & Roberts, 1861.

State Papers Domestic of the Reign of Elizabeth, 1870.

Stjerna, K., *Women & the Reformation*, Malden, MA/Oxford: Blackwell, 2009.

Strype, J., *Ecclesiastical Memorials*, Oxford: Clarendon Press, 1816.

Taylor, J., *Lucifer's Lackey*, 1640.

Warner, H., *Alone of All Her Sex – The Myth and the Cult of the Virgin Mary*, Oxford: OUP, 1976.

Weissberger, B. F. (ed.), *Queen Isabel I of Castile – Power, Patronage, Persona*, Woodbridge: Tamesis, 2008.

Wiesner, M. E., *Women and Gender in Early Modern Europe*, Cambridge: CUP, 2008.

Whitelock, A., *Mary Tudor, England's First Queen*, London: Bloomsbury, 2009.

Wiesner-Hanks, M. (ed.), *Converts Confronting Reformation: Catholic and Protestant Nuns in Germany*, Milwaukee: Marquette University Press, 1996.

Wilson, D., *A Tudor Tapestry: Men, Women and Society in Reformation England*, Pittsburgh, PA: University of Pittsburgh Press, 1972.

Wilson, K. M. (ed.), *Women Writers of the Renaissance and Reformation*, Atlanta, GA: University of Georgia Press, 1987.

Zimmermann, K. (ed.), *Luther's Letters to Women*, London: Chapman and Hall, 1865.

INDEX